Wheels, Waves, Wings and Drums

Wheels, Waves, Wings and Drums

My Twentieth Century Journey

by

Peter Beatson

Order this book online at www.trafford.com
or email orders@trafford.com

Most Trafford titles are also available at major online book retailers.

Printed in the United States of America.

ISBN: 978-1-4269-4167-2 (sc)
ISBN: 978-1-4269-4168-9 (hc)
ISBN: 978-1-4269-4169-6 (e)

Library of Congress Control Number: 2010912065

*Our mission is to efficiently provide the world's finest, most comprehensive book publishing
service, enabling every author to experience success. To find out how to publish your
book, your way, and have it available worldwide, visit us online at www.trafford.com*

Trafford rev. 09/21/2010

 www.trafford.com

North America & international
toll-free: 1 888 232 4444 (USA & Canada)
phone: 250 383 6864 ♦ fax: 812 355 4082

I dedicate this book

to

My father, John Humphrey Beatson
for the opportunity to advance my education

The Reverend Sam Taylor
for forthrightness and friendship
in my formative years

Wing Commander C.J. Hackett
for encouragement and for mentoring me
in medical services

Acknowledgements

This book presented many unforeseen challenges. I owe my thanks and gratitude to all those who have assisted me in bringing it to completion:

Elaine Balpataky, who patiently ploughed through the audiotapes I had made over a period of several years, transcribed them onto the typed page, and organized them into chapters.

My daughter, Jacqueline Hughes, who assisted with transcribing, editing, fact checking and writing for permissions.

Mary Stevens, who encouraged me at the beginning to start the project, saying that it was a worthwhile thing to do, and who also assisted with the transcription.

Dan Wilkens, who scanned and digitized the photographs and postcards.

Mike Skinner of Tillsonburg Commercial Printers, who finalized the scanning and retrieval of images.

Table of Contents

List of Illustrations

Chapter IX

Photo Credits

Most of the 72 images contained in this book are photographs from the Beatson family archives or photographs taken by the author himself. Exceptions are:

- ♣ Chapter III: S.S. *Anselm,* originally from a Booth Line postcard issued by the company, circa 1935. Retrieved in 2010 from http://www.wartimememories.co.uk/ships/anselm.html
- ♣ Chapter III: H.M.S. *Challenger,* copied from a tea card enclosed in a package of Red Rose_Blue Ribbon Tea, by Brooke Bond Foods Ltd., Montreal, Canada, n.d.
- ♣ Chapter III: map of Sierra Leone, West Africa, retrieved from The Central Intelligence Agency's *The World Factbook* (public domain) at https://www.cia.gov/library/publications/the-world-factbook/
- ♣ Chapter IV: photograph of Peter Beatson, by an unknown African photographer, Freetown, Sierra Leone, 1942
- ♣ Chapter IV: Planes flown out of Hastings Airfield, Sierra Leone: Lockheed Hudson; Fairey Swordfish; and Walrus, have been used courtesy of Ted Nevill at Cody Images.
- ♣ Chapter V: Black Combe viewed from Silecroft, near Millom in Cumberland. Copied from Sankeys Barrow postcard, circa 1950

- Chapter VI: "Forthcoming Entertainments," N.A.A.F.I. Club Sleaford. Photograph of a poster advertising upcoming events, circa 1944
- Chapter VI: N.A.A.F.I. Club, Sleaford. Copy of postcard published for Navy, Army and Airforce Institutes, by The Photochrom Co. Ltd., London and Tunbridge Wells, circa 1944
- Chapter VII: I.C.I. Plant where Peter worked. Copied from *Pharmaceutical Research in I.C.I., 1936–57*, p. 8. Imperial Chemical Industries, Pharmaceutical Division, 1957. Printed by the Kynoch Press, Birmingham, U.K.
- Chapter VII: Macclesfield, Cheshire. Copy of a postcard with pen sketch by L.A. Buckley, date and printer unknown
- Chapter VII: Rainow Village, Cheshire. Copy of a greeting card featuring an original painting by Ian Price, c1984. A "Prince Studio Card," printed by Poynton, Cheshire, U.K.

Cover images:

Permission to use the image of the R.A.F. badge was given by Kevin Corti. The image was retrieved from his website at www.kevincorti.com

The image of the Fairey Swordfish on the field was retrieved from Wikipedia Commons at http://en.wikipedia.org

The image of the Fairey Swordfish in flight has been used courtesy of Ted Nevill at Cody Images.

The image of the S.S. *Anselm* was retrieved from http://www.wartimememories.co.uk/ships/anselm.html

Chapter I

I was born in Warrington, England, on September 26, 1919, at 148 Battersby Lane, not far from the army barracks where my uncle worked. My father had just come out of the army after serving in the First World War. He had been involved in the fiasco at Gallipoli, where luckily he had escaped with his life. He had then been evacuated to the island of Limnos and eventually to Alexandria, Egypt, along with a lot of Australian and New Zealand troops. The goal of the operation had been to land on Gallipoli and open up a sort of second front, but the Turks were already aware of what was going to happen, and as the ships came on shore and the troops landed on the beach, the Turks simply shelled them unmercifully from higher positions established in advance.

Peter's father, John Humphrey Beatson, 1918.

Alexandria, Egypt: hospital that housed Peter's father and other Gallipoli survivors.

I wasn't particularly well as a child. I had pyloric stenosis in the abdomen. When I swallowed, the food kept coming back up. Eventually my father said, "Well this is not getting anywhere. We had better go to a specialist in Manchester."

That meant going from Warrington to Manchester to see a top-line doctor who did an operation on my abdomen. In 1919, as you can imagine, it wasn't as simple or precise as it would be today. However, they fixed me up—got the valve doing its thing—and I came back home to Battersby Lane. From then on I seemed to be okay—I was lucky. The scar is pretty enormous, however, and has stayed with me for the rest of my life.

Before the war, my father had been a teacher. After the war, he secured a job in the Botany Department at the University of Manchester, which was then called Owen's College. So we moved from Warrington to a house on Winsford Road in Fallowfield, Manchester. It was a small council house with a big problem. It seems there had been a limestone pit under the house at the time of its construction. Consequently the house was terribly damp and really unfit to live in. My father, a keen gardener, made a nice little garden there. My mother—who was pretty determined, not letting go too easily when she got her teeth into something—played heck with the Council. She had the inspectors come around to see the dampness that was constantly coming up the wall. Obviously this dampness wasn't any good for me, being "delicate" so called.

During that time, there was a lady across the road, a Mrs. Law, who used to babysit me when my Mum and Dad went out to dances or elsewhere. The Laws were very nice people. I used to see Mr. Law going out to work very smartly dressed, with black bowler hat, black suit, white cuffs and tie—a smart gentleman, smartly dressed, smartly walking down the road to work. One time he made a radio set for us. It was a two-valve or two-tube model, and I remember looking into it years later—wonderfully engraved wooden cabinet, and the wires were perfect, straight along and at right angles. We had that set for years. It wasn't until the Second World War that I realized why he had been so professional in making it. I was going down Moss Side looking for bits for my motorcycle, and there on a little shop I saw

"Mr. Law, Funeral Director." So that was why he walked out so smartly dressed in his black suit. That was why he was able to make such a wonderful cabinet for our wireless—he was an expert at carving coffins!

Eventually we left Winsford Road and moved to another house which would be better for me. It was a better house, but still a council house on Wilbraham Road. I remember that the very first time I went to school, Wilbraham Road was closed off, with gates at either end, between which the elite of Manchester lived—people with lots of money, huge houses and servants. We would walk to school up Wilbraham Road, in and out through the gates near Holy Innocents Church and into our school. Very soon, however, they built a road through, and the gates were removed. Eventually they built a tram track.

Tram fare for children in those days was a penny. My mother used to put me on the tram to go up Wilbraham Road, a distance of about two-and-one-half miles, to my school. The trams were electrically driven with overhead wires and only four wheels. They were double-deckers, open at the front, both upstairs and down. The middle part was enclosed with glass, and I used to go upstairs and sit right at the front where there was a wind, and where the tram would be bobbing up and down, which I found exciting. Sometimes I would make it upstairs, but other times the conductor who collected the money at the bottom of the stairs wouldn't let me go up—too dangerous. The driver was downstairs in the open part at the front of the tram, and when he reached the terminus, he would go to the other end and drive the tram back the other way. When we reached the end, the guard used to get out and pull the huge trolley down with a pole and hook, walk round with it, and put it on the overhead wire at the other end. Then back we would go. It was quite a thrill for me as a youngster to go to school that way.

When I went to school, sometimes I'd walk home and save my penny car fare to buy aniseed balls or sweets. There was a little tuck shop right opposite the school, run by a couple of what

I thought were older people. You could buy aniseed balls and gobstoppers for a ha'penny. I went to primary school at Mosely Road, a glazed red brick building, quite large with two storeys, one section for the boys and another for the girls. As I recall, it had a red tiled roof and a rounded dome with a point on the top. The school had been built between 1911 and 1914, and my brother, David, tells me it has since been torn down.

The first teacher I remember was a Miss Buckley when I was five years old. She was a nice young person, a gentle person, and we had her for the first year. In the second year, however, at the age of six, we had a Miss Clegg, a real battle-axe—an old-time teacher with severe-looking clothes and hair pulled back into a bun. She made sure you knew your alphabet and your times tables. She'd make you stand up in your place in the class and recite the times table—or whatever it happened to be.

On one occasion during the winter, I must have had a cold; I didn't feel well at all, but Miss Clegg made me go out to the playground anyway. I remember feeling pretty "ropey," but nothing much after that. When I woke up, I was in my own bed at home—with pneumonia. Of course, there were no antibiotics or sulpha drugs at the time; so I had kaolin poultice and camphorated oil on my chest. I must have been pretty sick because I remember my mother and father kneeling at the foot of my bed praying. I guess they were praying for my survival, though I didn't really know how sick I was at the time. I did recover, and went back to school, presumably with extra special care.

I don't remember too much after that until 1926, the year of the General Strike. Conditions in Britain at that time were pretty miserable. The First World War was over, nobody had work, and the political situation was chaotic. The public was up in arms about it, and there was a General Strike. The trams stopped running; the policemen and the railways were on strike; nobody was working. I don't know how long it lasted, but I do remember difficulties getting home from school. A few people had cars, and they would give children a ride and drop them off at the nearest point so that they could walk home. Even at that time, I was interested in cars, and so I used to try to ride in a different car each day—put my thumb up and flag a different one down. I rode in a Rolls Royce one day, and in something else the next. I remember teachers from the University doing the policeman's job of point duty—directing traffic this way and that at intersections. There were no traffic lights in those days.

I stayed at Mosely Road School until I was 11 in 1928. I missed writing the Eleven Plus exam because I had been sick. I was a mischievous child. I remember one incident particularly well. There was a funny little store on Platt Lane, a bit like a variety store. The proprietor was an African named Neurerka, and you could buy all sorts of things from him, including stink bombs. These stink bombs were sold in tiny, round chip boxes with sawdust inside. The boxes contained tiny glass vials of hydrogen sulfide, which smells like rotten eggs. I bought three of them and took the first to the cinematograph room at school and dropped it off the balustrade down some stone steps. We couldn't smell it in the cinematograph room, where we were viewing an educational film, but the smell drifted up into the main hall where they had to abandon singing lessons. I also put a stink bomb in the cloak room, thinking that one of the boys would take the smell home in his cloak at lunch time. I put the third one by a Wall's Ice Cream cart at the school gates. We used to buy snow fruit, a sort of Popsicle, there for a penny. Sometimes the vendors would cut the snow fruit in half and allow us to buy one for a ha'penny, but the current vendor would not; so I decided to punish him with the stink bomb. Unfortunately, as I tossed the empty box into the bushes near the school, somebody in my class saw me and spilled the beans. Big trouble. The whole school knew who had done the mischief. They had a big assembly the next day at 9:00 o'clock, before we went to our separate classrooms. I was hauled in front of the whole school, and the headmaster, Roberts, laid on the strap really hard in front of everyone.

Well, this played right into the hands of the bumptious class master who had it in for me. He was a young, tall, self-opinionated bore, and had been a student of my father at the university. I don't know whether my father had been exasperated with him—I can well imagine that he might have been—but this teacher gave me a really hard time. On one occasion we had to give lectures on two topics of our choosing (we were all under the age of 11). I gave one talk on South America and the Amazon, because the subject interested me, and another on motor cars, because I had a lot of information in the *Wonder Book of Motor Cars*. Both the students and the teacher questioned me on the topic, and he tried very hard to trip me up, but he didn't succeed. When the Eleven Plus exam came, I scraped through, and he was cross about that too. If you didn't pass the Eleven Plus you had to stay in primary school until you were 14, and your opportunities for advancement would be nil. However, I did manage to pass by the skin of my teeth.

During my time at Mosely Road School, there used to be fights—fisticuff fights—meaning with bare fists. Word would be passed around that so-and-so was to fight so-and-so at a particular playground at lunchtime. I would try to get out of this, but you had to go. Some of the guys were quite big or were good boxers, whereas I wasn't great in stature and so I got a real pasting from some of these boys. I must have said something to my father, for he bought me a punch ball on elastics from floor to ceiling, and showed me how to box. I practised punching this thing and then we had somebody arrange a fight for "Beetroot," as they called me. I was to fight Ronald Parker, a big guy. At any rate, I did quite well and he was getting the worst of it. Instead of carrying on with the boxing, however, he decided to use his boots. (Kids in those days went to school wearing laced-up boots.) He kicked me in a place where it really hurts, and somebody told the Headmaster about it. So I had to go to the Headmaster's office and show him the damage. It was really bleeding—not a nice situation. So Mr. Garlic, a form master, had this lad out and strapped him—laid into him something terrible. I guess he must have learned to fight fairly after that, as I had no further trouble with him. I had a few problems with another boy named Vincent Haskell, but then it died out, and we moved on to playing marbles in the schoolyard.

After Mosely Road, I went to Didsbury Central School. It was nicely situated, a little more out of town towards West Didsbury and opposite the Capitol Cinema theatre. It had a playing field, a track, and a football field, where we played cricket and soccer. I used to run on the track to see how long it took me to run a mile—of course, I never got it below five minutes. It was a good school for sports, but some of the teaching wasn't all that great. We had an English teacher who was very funny, a math teacher who was very severe, and a French teacher who was a brute.

The English teacher, a young man, would teach us and then read a passage from a book, *Night Watches*, by W. W. Jacobs. These were stories about a night watchman who was on the wharves in London when the ships came in. He'd tell stories about the sailors who'd come to spend time on shore and then go back to sea with no money left. There were many characters, all with different names—one was called Sandy Russell. The stories were hilarious. I went to the Library, not far from where we lived on Platt Lane, and I borrowed all the W.W. Jacobs books in turn. I'd be reading them and suddenly burst out laughing and my Mum would ask, "What are you laughing at? What are you laughing at?"

As I said earlier, my French teacher was a brute. We sat in rows doing our work. He would come up behind us and look over our shoulders, and if we weren't doing the work correctly, he'd bang us across our ears and knock us into the guy in the next seat. WANG! He was pretty heavy with the ruler, too. I think one of the parents must have complained to the school. My Dad had known him previously at the night school where my father was teaching. At any rate, the Headmaster called me in and asked, "What's going on?" At first I wouldn't tell him, but eventually I explained the situation. The teacher was gone the next day—right out of the school. They didn't want him around any more.

We played cricket at Didsbury, and I enjoyed that. At the time, there was an Australian cricketer named Larwood who always bowled the body, and never the wicket. He struck fear into everybody. We had one boy in the class who thought he was Larwood. He used to bowl at the body and try to injure you. So I thought, "Okay, I'll learn how to play left-handed. So I played left-handed bat and blocked every ball he sent down. He got really choked up with this. He was whizzing one down to me one day, and it seemed to be timed just right. I went down on one knee—as I'd seen other cricketers doing—and I didn't really have to do anything. I just scooped it, and it went right over Parswood Road into the construction site for the Capitol Theatre. That was the highlight of my cricket career!

At Didsbury, we had one hour for lunch. I had a bicycle; so I used to ride home, which was quite a way from the school. I would have 20 minutes to ride home, 20 minutes to gobble my lunch, and 20 minutes to ride back. The only problem was that Mother never had my lunch ready. Time didn't seem to register too much with her. So I ate lunch at home for awhile, but eventually resorted to taking sandwiches to school. One day when I was riding my bike to school—a Sunbeam that I had bought for five shillings—I was standing on the pedals because I was late, when the front down tube on the bicycle frame broke and snapped off, and I went sprawling. I was hurt, but nevertheless wheeled the bike to school and told them what had happened. The teacher didn't believe me though, and I was very disappointed after all that effort.

At Didsbury Central, we had a concert where everybody had to do something on stage. I had been rehearsing a song entitled, "I took my harp to a party, but nobody asked me to play." The lady next door could play the piano; so she went through it with me until I performed it reasonably well. When my turn came to sing,

I was nervous, and I started off without looking at the audience. I was halfway through my song when I noticed one of my teachers laughing his head off. It was my math teacher, who was usually a miserable sort of guy, and I had never seen him laugh in my life. He was laughing so hard that I forgot my words! That's all I can remember about Didsbury School, a place where I didn't get on very well.

John and Florence Beatson with Peter and younger brother, David, 1931.

Platt Fields Park, Manchester: model boats that taught Peter to sail.

Young Peter paddling a rented canoe.

My next school was Hulme Grammar School, which was situated in the other direction on Princess Road. It was established in 1890 and was more like a private college, but they did take some regular pupils. I found the teaching there totally different from Didsbury. It was interesting, and the teachers were good—not totally lenient, but good. As a result, I began to enjoy my lessons and made good progress. However, I still didn't do very well at math because I had a lousy teacher. He was an avid climber who used to go on and on about his climbing experiences in the Lake District. Some of the boys didn't mind this at first, but when it got closer to exams, one of them stood up and suggested that he had better get on with the work. This teacher didn't last—he was told to leave—but I continued to be terrible at mathematics for a long time.

My English teacher at Hulme Grammar School was a Scot named Anderson. He'd been a colonel in the army in the First World War. We called him "Tin Belly" because he'd been wounded in the stomach and had a tin plate—or so we were told. He was a fiercesome guy, and what he said was "It." When he came into the classroom, we would shut up—we wouldn't say a word because he had been used to army discipline. However, he was a good teacher, and consequently I did quite well in English.

Our chemistry teacher was a young guy, not long out of college. He presented chemistry and biology in a very interesting way. He was a really good teacher, and I related to him well. In my class, there was a boy named Appleyard whose father was a dentist. He and I were always vying for the top spot in chemistry.

There was a wonderful playing field at Hulme Grammar School where they played rugby in the winter and lacrosse and cricket in the summer. In those days, sports were compulsory. We had classes from Monday to Friday, with Wednesday afternoon off. We also had classes on Saturday morning. On Wednesday and Saturday afternoons, however, there were compulsory games. I played rugby for one season, but I wasn't very good. I was fast, but not heavy. In one game, a guy couldn't quite catch me; so he grabbed the back of my collar, and we both tumbled over and over. I broke my collar bone; so that was the end of rugby for that season. However, if you didn't participate in a sport, you had to work on stage construction for a major concert held every year. You couldn't get out of it: you still had to go to school on Wednesday and Saturday afternoons. This left very little time for homework, and even less time for yourself.

On one occasion, we went to Manchester Athletic grounds and there we spotted our chemistry teacher. Boy, could he ever run! After that we had even more respect for him. The history teacher was mediocre; the chemistry teacher was good, and the math teacher was useless. English was good, but woodwork was a disaster because the teacher had no patience. Everyone had to have a project finished by the end of the term. I was making a bathroom cabinet, and I couldn't get the front panel right on the cabinet door. I hated woodwork then, and I haven't been wild about it since. Even today metal work is okay, but woodwork—forget it! These experiences carry through from the time you are at school.

Hulme Grammar School had a cadet corps. At age 16, I joined the Officers' Training Corps (O.T.C.). The younger boys were cadets, with drills and parades, and they had to use these old Boer War rifles—very long-stemmed things. When you moved up into the O.T.C., you were issued the short Lee Endfield rifles that were used by the army of the day. One summer, we went for a two-week summer camp. We camped in bell tents overlooking Grange-over-Sands. We had group marches up and down the hills at the back of Grange. It was a hot summer, and we had to wear full khaki dress, the regular stuff that the army wore: the boots, the puttees, and the Lee Endfield rifles, along with backpacks. The officers would walk in front with a cane, setting the pace. It was hard work, but I suppose it didn't do us any harm.

One day during the camp, I spied two of our cadets out in a boat at Grange-over-Sands. (There was a lot more water in the bay than there is today.) They had taken a rowboat out and had thrown the anchor over the side, then couldn't get the anchor back up. The tide was rising and was beginning to pull the nose of the boat down. I ran to the man who had rented the boat and said, "Look at that." He got a boat out and was messing around with it. So I said, "Give me a boat, NOW!" I rowed out to them, and got there just in time. I used the bayonet on my Enfield rifle to cut the anchor rope, and got the boys back safely to shore, where I gave them a penny lecture. It wouldn't have been too long before the boat would have been pulled under.

During those years, I used to go to Holy Innocents Church where I sang in the choir. The vicar was the Rev'd Sam Taylor. You couldn't sit through one of his sermons without taking notice. You never went to sleep. He was excellent, and I was going twice a day—morning and evening to sing in the choir. As a result, I was fairly tuned in to passages in the Bible. At Hulme Grammar School we also got one lesson a week of Religious Instruction (R.I.). At the end of the term they posted our names and our marks on a sheet on the wall. I remember that Anderson, the Scot, whom the students called "Tin Belly," looked at the sheet and said, "Whose little joke is this then?" I was top in R.I. He said, "If you can be top in R.I., you can be top in English as well. (I was fifth at the time.)

It was an interesting time. Most kids walked or rode to school on a bike. However, there was one boy whose father was a dentist. He came to school in a Morgan car with a four-cylinder engine— like a sports car, a bit like an MG. Boy, we thought that was something! This was about 1934 or 1935.

I got to know Teddy Bates at this school. We used to walk home together, and we shared hobbies like radio. Opposite the school was a very large house where a professional man lived—I can't remember whether he was a doctor or dentist. At any rate, he was also a radio ham. I don't know how we got to know him, but we went across and he showed us all his equipment. His wife may have been house-proud, because he had all his radio equipment in a roll-top desk, with the power supply underneath because it tended to be physically quite big in those days. He would open the desk top, and there it all was. Rather neat—it didn't spoil the drawing room in any shape or fashion. Both of us became interested in amateur radio at that point. We also tried playing musical instruments. Ted had a saxophone, and I had a clarinet, but neither of us made much progress with them.

We did build a radio, however, a tube set, a one-valve set. We had nothing to construct it in, so we used one of the slatted wooden boxes that oranges came in at the time. You had to have holes for a shaft to go through for the knobs, so we used a red hot poker to burn the holes because we didn't have a drill. We built crystal sets first, and then a one-valve set. We'd buy a valve or tube for a sixpence from a second-hand shop in Sherwood St. on Friday night when we got our sixpence spends. By Saturday night we'd have blown it by making the wrong connections, so we'd have to wait until the next Friday before we could go on the air again. Ted must have read something about putting a fuse in, and it was only a matter of a penny for a fuse, so we learnt a bit that way. In Wilbraham Road we had domestic radio, and everyone had to have a pole for their antenna. The poles were like flag poles with round discs at the top. I used to attach my amateur listening radio to ours.

One of Peter's early photographs (long exposure).

Telsen Radiogram in the Beatson home circa 1930.

Holy Innocents Church, Fallowfield,
where Peter sang in the choir.

Manchester, England: Hulme Grammar School.

During the same period, Ted and I got an old motor bike from somewhere. I can't remember what it cost, but it must have been cheap. It was a 1923 BSA hand change, with a round gas tank like a cylinder. We pulled it all to bits, put it back together and rode it around. There was a Wilbraham Association, like a community association, with a cinder track around it. After we put the cycle together we rode it around on this track. It had a lever throttle—not a twist grip throttle—and you had to push a lever up to get it to go faster. We ran it around only a few times. I don't think the exhaust was any good, and it made such a racket that a lady came storming out of one of the houses. Her husband worked nights, as a policeman; so we didn't push our luck in that direction. However, we did learn a lot with this motor bike about how to put a bike together. We learned only a little bit about how to ride one.

I had another friend over on the other side of Wilbraham Road who owned a bicycle. One day I asked him, "Can you lend me your bicycle to ride to Timperley?" He said "Yes," so I borrowed it once or twice. Then he got a little awkward about it. He said, "You can borrow my bicycle if you let me borrow your air gun." I had an air rifle that I used to shoot at targets in our back yard. I wasn't too keen on lending it, but I wanted badly to go to Timperly to visit my friend, so I said, "All right. But you be careful with this thing—don't point it at anybody. Only shoot it in my back yard at a board." When I returned from Timperly, I found out that he'd shot it—not at the target in my back yard—but at a little girl from a distance across the field. Luckily the slug was just about spent, and though it hit her in the forehead, it only made a weal. Of course her parents came storming around. I promised them he'd never see that rifle again, and I pleaded with them not to tell the police. I thought I had them convinced, but they called the police anyway. Both my Dad and Mum were home when the police came to the door—a disaster in those days. My Dad got really wild. He broke the rifle into pieces in front of the policeman and started laying into me. The policeman said, "No. No. Don't do that." So that was the end of the air rifle. Of course I never borrowed the bike again either. Not long after that, the time came for me to leave school. I left a year earlier than Ted, who was in the class a year behind me.

Chapter II

When it came time to go to work, I took a job with a radio firm on Bridge St. in Manchester called Holiday & Hemmerdinger. I had always been interested in radio, and their business was to repair radios that had gone defunct. However, once of my first assignments was a rather unusual one. In November 1936, King Edward VIII decided to abdicate, and his abdication speech was scheduled to be broadcast. At the same time, there was a big occasion at Manchester's Midland Hotel where many of the guests wished to hear the speech. I was given the task of holding a microphone in front of a radio loudspeaker and an amplifier in the large hall so that the hotel guests could hear the King's voice. Other employees of the radio firm were sent elsewhere to do the same thing. Shortly after the abdication speech, there would be the proclamation of King George VI when bells were to ring throughout the country. However, the bells at Manchester Town Hall had been sent away for casting. So I was assigned to the belfry with a dual turntable to play recordings of the Westminster Bells to be relayed to speakers on the lamp posts in Albert Square. In fact, the proclamation of George VI was read from the Town Hall steps using the same set up.

Nearly all the radios at Holiday & Hemmerdinger were tube radios, as the ones operated by 220 volts were just coming into being. I started in repairs, but then the firm took an agency for American tubes (or valves as they call them in Britain). They would import and sell them, and of course, someone had to pack them. At first the office typist was the designated packer, but then the job fell to me, as the last one hired, I suppose.

I did the packing for awhile, but then I thought, "This is getting me nowhere. I'm not learning anything about radios." So I went to the management and said, "This is no good. If you want somebody to pack tubes, hire a fourteen-year-old right out of school." (Some students at that time, at primary, did finish at age 14.) "Hire somebody like that and let them do it." Well they gave the packing work back to the typist, but she didn't want to do it, and after a couple of days, it got piled back onto me. So I thought, "That's it! I had better go looking for something else."

Eric Peter Beatson 1937.

I started looking for another job, but it was hard to know what to look for, and I didn't see any radio jobs in the offing. I did, however, see an ad for somebody to look after a sales room in the warehouse at W.&H. Pownall, a clothing manufacturer on Stockport Road in Manchester. I knew Mr. Pownall, the owner, had a reputation for being a big bear. Even my mother had heard of him when she went from Warrington by train to work in Manchester. Nevertheless, I applied for and got the job.

In any manufacturing business there are always seconds—things with flaws in them. This company was shipping their seconds to Africa—to people who apparently didn't mind the flaws. Of course, this merchandise would have to be sold at the right price. My job would be to organize that process. I had to collect all the orders, put them in big wicker skips, load them onto a two-wheeled dolly (they were pretty heavy), and then dolly them to the shipping department where they would be checked off. I got a shilling for every £100 of value (not 100 pounds of weight). So I managed to raise my wage from the basic 15 shillings a week to 17 shillings and sixpence—by working hard and getting rid of this stuff.

It just so happened that the girl who was receiving these goods from me was nice looking. On one occasion, we chatted a bit, and I said, "Would you like to come out with me—pictures or something?" (That was always a favourite, to go to the cinema.) Winnie Murphy was her name—a nice girl—and we went to the pictures a couple of times. However, her father was manager of a dirt-track motorcycle team at Bellevue, and he was moved to Norwich (U.K.). We wrote to each other a couple of times, but that was the end of that little episode.

I worked at Pownall's for awhile, but eventually decided to move to another Manchester warehouse called J.&N. Phillips. So I said to my manager at Pownall's, "Tell Mr. Pownall that I'm leaving and that I would like to give a week's notice."

"I'm not telling him! Tell him yourself," he responded.

I could see that he was afraid, though a big, grown man, and I was only 17 or 18. He handed me the internal phone after saying, "Beatson wants to speak to you, Sir."

"Oh, it's Beatson here. I want to leave. I'd like to give a week's notice."

Deathly silence—then a big roar, "Nobody gives me notice! I WON'T be given notice! NOBODY gives me notice!" Then something like, "Take a week's money and go—NOW!"

That suited me just fine. Pownall had the reputation for being a madman. Once during a fire, he had been seen rampaging up and down Stockport Road, waving his hands about like a lunatic. He owned a nice house in Wilmslow, where the maintenance men from his firm would work from time to time.

So I went to J.&N. Phillips, a similar sort of warehouse, but more peaceable. They didn't manufacture anything—they just bought and sold. I didn't stay very long, however. I looked at the men working next to me and saw that they wore shabby suits with frayed cuffs and pant bottoms—married guys with maybe one or two children, who had been working there for ages, and were earning only £3.10 per week. I knew that I was going nowhere and so I started to look around for another job. Eventually—I believe it was around 1938—I found one that really interested me.

I applied for a job at Boots the Chemist in Sale. When they interviewed me, they asked what I had done and what I was good at. I replied that I had done quite well in chemistry in school; so they gave me a job as a pharmaceutical apprentice. This job was better in so many ways: it wasn't far from where we were living in Sale, and more importantly, it was a job where you were looking towards a career. We worked from 9:00 a.m. until 8:00 p.m., with half days on Wednesdays. On Saturdays, however, we worked from 9:00 a.m. until 9:00 p.m., so I really didn't have much time for myself. In addition to work, I had homework because I was taking classes from the head office in Nottingham. Sometimes after working and doing my homework, I would get on my bike and ride around Carrington. It would be pitch black, of course, but I just had to get some fresh air in my lungs.

In spite of the long hours, the job was interesting and the people were interesting. The pharmacist was also very helpful. We had to make up all the prescriptions then and there, as there were no drugs in bottles already prepared. We had to make them individually, one bottle of pills or one jar of ointment at a time. The theory was that if we were to pre-prepare things in bulk, then any mistakes would carry through to more people. In those days, the inspector would come around, without telling you he was the inspector. He would hand you a prescription, and when you had to make it up, he would put half of it in his own bottle and take it away for analysis, leaving you with the other half. It had better be right or you were in big trouble. We never got into trouble like that, although sometimes our work was difficult because the doctor's handwriting wasn't the best, and the darned prescriptions were in Latin anyway. For some you just had to pluck up your courage and phone the doctor. All in all, though, the work was good and I learned a lot.

On one occasion, the pharmacist asked me to go to the swimming baths with his kids. These nine and ten-year-olds could swim across the pool, whereas I, at 18, couldn't swim at all, even though I had been taken to swimming lessons by my father. Well, this time I was really shamed into it. There was no way I was going to let these kids discover I was unable to swim. So I swam right off!

I remember another funny incident at the pharmacy with one of the girls who worked on the cosmetic counter. She wasn't a bad looking girl—page boy hair cut, blonde—but a bit hoity-toity. She had been going out with some guy, and something, I don't know what, must have happened. Anyway, I was up in the men's lunch room doing my lessons when I heard her next door in the ladies' lunch room crying her eyes out. So I went in and asked her, "What's the matter?" She just kept on crying. The next week the same thing happened again. I couldn't get a word out of her, and I couldn't do my own studying. Well I took one of the tall, half-gallon, enamel jugs that were kept in the lunch room (originally to bring back ale from the pub), filled it up with water to the blue rim around the top, and tipped it right over her head as she sat there at the table. She stopped crying and never cried at work again. The manager chided me, "You shouldn't have done that." But I think he was glad I had because it stopped that nonsense. Not a very good introduction to girls, however!

This brings to mind another incident. One evening, about 7:00 o'clock, when the girls on the cosmetic and surgical counter had gone home, I was working alone at the counter when a really nice looking girl came in to purchase her monthly requirements. She had darkish hair and eyes, and she was wearing one of those black pork-pie hats that Princess Marina used to wear in those days. I went all red in the face, as I used to do, but I did serve her and survived that one. Lo and behold she came back the next month, and we had a little titter about this. Think of the times! It was 1938, and young men weren't as forward about things as they are now. Anyway, I said to her, "Would you like to come out?" She answered, "Yes. Okay." So we arranged to meet at the cinema in Stretford, a nice, big cinema. She came dressed like somebody out of a bandbox, and we enjoyed a lovely evening. We went out maybe two or three times after that. Later when I joined Armed Forces, I asked her if she would mind if I wrote to her. She said, "No. That's okay." She gave me her photograph and we wrote back and forth. Eventually, however, the letters became few and far between, and things sort of dribbled away to nothing.

A few years later, when I was with the Fleet Air Arm in West Africa, I was chatting with a guy who asked me where I was from. I said, "Sale," and lo and behold, he lived next door to this girl. He wrote home and learned that she'd been going out with an airman with a car—a little more pull than I had on a bicycle. Of course for anyone to have a car in those days was something else. So I lost out on that one. What a shame.

While I was still in Sale, I went for a few lessons in ballroom dancing. At the time, if you went to a wedding party or something similar and you couldn't ballroom dance, you felt stupid. It was a sort of social requirement. So I went to a school of dancing with a friend named Norman. First, a man and a woman would demonstrate a particular dance, and then other helpers would take you onto the dance floor and show you how it was done. After the one-hour lesson you could stay on and join the regular dance. There were refreshments, and you could mix and socialize with people.

I remained at Sale and worked at Boots until I joined the Armed Forces. It was September 1939, and things were looking pretty dicey in Europe. Hitler had already occupied the Sudetenland, which he claimed belonged to him because it had been Germany's before the First World War. His military machine was getting enormous, and he thought the time opportune; so he invaded Poland. He hoped to gobble up Poland after nibbling off bits here and there and coming into an agreement with Mussolini in Italy. However, Britain and France had guaranteed that if Poland were attacked, they would lend their assistance. So war was declared.

My friend Norman, whose job was to deliver orders from the pharmacy on his bicycle, was called up right away, as he was already in the Territorial Army. When he came back on a visit, I was of two minds as to what I should do. I would get this sort of uneasy feeling at the back of my neck. I would see other people going and think that I should go. It wasn't quite a white feather feeling—of being a coward—it wasn't that bad, but I had this uneasy feeling that I should go and do my thing. However, when I went to the Army recruiting place in Manchester, they didn't want me because I had a medical background. So I thought, "The war will be over by Christmas anyway. I'll try the Air Force." So I grew a mustache and cooked my age by one year, and I was accepted.

When they asked me what I wanted to be, I replied, "I want to be a wireless operator." Then they asked me what I was currently doing. When I told them I was a pharmaceutical apprentice, they said, "You can't go in for a wireless operator—you have to go in the Medical." When I protested that I didn't want Medical, they said, "Go in the Medical first, and then you can re-muster when you get in," meaning that I could change my trade. I hadn't heard that one before. So I enlisted and then waited until January 29, 1940, when I got called. Things were pretty quiet at that time. Hitler had not yet invaded France, although he had pretty well devastated Poland. I was ordered to report to Cardington in Bedford, where the big airships were stationed and from where they flew JR100 British airships, but at the time it was a recruiting place.

Peter (left) and Walter Cross (centre) with an R.A.F. friend 1940.

It was also January, 1940, and very cold, with deep snow. I boarded the train at Manchester wearing only a raincoat and grey flannel trousers. I don't remember whether I wore a hat. It took 24 hours to do the 100–120 miles from Manchester to Bedford. The trains were steam-heated, but the steam never got back to the compartments. By the time we arrived, we were frozen stiff. We eventually got to Cardington in Bedford, where we were lined up in our civilian clothes for inoculations and a medical exam. As we stood in line, a sergeant was asking questions like, "Is this your name? Is this your age?"

"Oh no, they have my age wrong!"

I told him it was out by a year, and so I was able to have that corrected quietly. We also lined up for uniforms and were assigned to a hut.

There were about 26 people in each hut with two coke stoves in the middle of the room. The weather was still freezing and blowing like heck. I had a miserable time there. I had only half a crown (two shillings, sixpence); so I couldn't afford a cup of tea in the Navy, Army and Air Force canteen and buy a razor blade as well. Incidentally, my parents had given me the two shillings and six pence—not the Air Force. I would have to wait another 10–12 days before getting my first pay, which was 10 shillings and sixpence—for a week.

I remember my father saying, as he saw me off from Central Station in Manchester, "You don't really have to go because you are in a reserved occupation," referring to my work at the pharmacy. Certain occupations were classified as essential to the community, such as munitions factory workers and other trades essential to the war effort. I sometimes ask myself, "Why did you want to go?" "What psyche prompted you to want to go?" Excitement, I suppose. Adventure. The challenge to your courage. Things like that, though we didn't know just what a challenge it was going to be. My father, who had been in the First World War, rarely talked about it, although we knew he'd had a bad time. I guess it was the sense of "doing your duty" or trying to stamp out Hitler and his methods of treating people. Also there was the fear, justifiable indeed, that if England were overrun by Germany, we and our families would suffer greatly, as was the case in Europe. So what we had in the back of our minds was to defend our country against this scourge. "They also serve who only stand and wait." Sometimes you had to play an unglamourous part, where recognition didn't always make the headlines. Nevertheless those years were harrowing, exciting and satisfying times—it's hard to put a finger on it.

The man in the next bunk, Walter Cross, was from Birkenhead, and we struck up a friendship. We both got posted to Tangmere with Number 1 Squadron, Britain's elite fighter squadron. Tangmere was located on the south coast near Chichester. We were fortunate because the weather was warming up. It was 1940, at a time when none of the Air Force had yet gone to France. They had famous pilots like Cobber Kain, a Hurricane pilot from New Zealand, very daring. Unfortunately he was too daring. After shooting down a German plane, he did a victory roll too near the ground, crashed and was killed. Other famous names were Prince Obelensky and Sailor Malan, but I suppose, by now, most of them have been forgotten.

We were stationed at Tangmere where we did our drills and square bashing. The warrant officer who conducted our drills on the square was a short, dour Scotsman with an amazing voice that could be heard miles away. His regimental number, if I remember correctly, was 43. This meant he'd been in the Air Force for eons, and was probably due to be discharged just before the war started. The Royal Air Force (R.A.F.) had begun in the First World War as the Royal Flying Corps, and was attached to the army. Eventually, however, it became an entity unto itself called the Royal Air Force. Regimental numbers had been given since the beginning; so this guy with the number 43 had been in the R.A.F. for a long time. He was a very fiercesome guy while on the parade ground, but off the parade ground, he was quite affable.

There were flying sorties from Tangmere, the Number 1 squadron and the number one Air Force base on the south coast. My job was tending to the sick and injured. There wasn't much bombing in early 1940, so it was a relatively quiet time because Germany was looking east towards Poland. Eventually I was posted to Farnborough, although I don't know why. They must have needed some help.

Farnborough, near Aldershot, was the experimental station for new aircraft that were being tested and tried out. I worked in the sick quarters, and it was then that I saw my first plane crash.

It was a training aircraft, and the officer in the plane, a lieutenant, was injured. We rushed over to the crash site, the fire crew and ourselves, and there was a lot of blood about. I looked at it and vomited in the grass. It was the first real casualty I had seen. A corporal standing next to me said, "You'll be all right now." And I was. I turned around and got on with the job, and we got the guy out.

Peter (bottom left) with R.A.F. friends at Farnborough 1940.

I wasn't long in Farnborough, and I don't remember much. One minor incident involved the fact that I was small in stature. We had been issued some old Air Force uniforms, and mine was a choker; it wasn't a collar-and-tie sort of thing, but went way up the neck. It was army type, but blue, and included a peaked forage cap. We were entitled to two uniforms, so I managed to get a second one of the blue collar-and-tie type, which I wore when I went out on special occasions. The other one I wore around the airfield. Some time later, I was granted leave and went back to Sale. I visited the shop where I had worked, and everyone was glad to see me. There was a nice-looking girl in the group, who worked in the library. So I asked the usual, would she like to go for an evening somewhere. To my surprise, she said, "Yes." I picked her up where she lived, and we went by bus or taxi to the Palace in Manchester, a theatre on Oxford Street. Girls in those days didn't go out dressed in jeans or baggy pants; they came dressed beautifully. Anyway she turned up and she really looked like a princess. She had very dark hair, and wore a pink, mid-length dress with a white cape. We went to the Palace where Nat Gonella was playing. A trumpet player, he had a dance band that toured around the country. When he started to do a solo performance of "Georgia," the whole place became quiet. Suddenly, from outside in the street, we heard the Salvation Army band marching by, "Babam, babam, babam." He just broke down laughing. Then after awhile, he picked it up again.

When the show ended we headed down the stairs to the street. It was just like a movie set. Here I was descending the stairs with this lovely girl on my arm. Then I saw looking up at me, a warrant officer from the camp in Farnborough. I watched his jaw sag, then drop right down to his neck. I think it was a combination of seeing me in my military cap—which I shouldn't have been wearing—and seeing me coming down the stairs with my lovely date. He didn't say anything, and I just smiled as we went by. I can still see that poor guy's face. I took the girl home, but nothing ever came of that. It was just a friendship, but it was also an interesting episode.

I returned to Farnborough for a few weeks, then was posted to Halton, near Aylsbury in Buckinghamshire. It was a big area camp and also a military hospital. We had to go to Nurses' Orderly Training, which lasted for quite a few weeks. There we were taught First Aid nursing and caring for the injured. We also learned about tropical diseases. We knew that we would be going abroad. I don't remember a great deal about the course, but obviously it was one that was needed. I met Walter (Bud) Cross again, as he was on the same course at the same time.

Following the course, we were to be posted to various locations in the U.K. While at Farnborough, I had volunteered to go with a squadron heading out to defend Norway, but they wouldn't let me go because I hadn't been at it long enough. At any rate, when our course was over, we had some choice as to where we wanted to go. I chose Sealand, Chester, because it wasn't far from Sale where my Mum and Dad lived. Walter Cross picked the same station because his family lived in Birkenhead in Tranmere, where he had worked at Lever Brothers. So we were both posted to Sealand.

The only memorable thing about that time is that I celebrated my 21st birthday there. A group of us got on our bicycles and cycled up and down the street at Connah's Quay, shouting and blowing whistles. We also had a few beers in the pubs—up one side and back down the other. There was no birthday cake or anything—just the magic of a 21st birthday. After that things went on in a very routine way. Bud Cross had a girlfriend he was keen on and who worked at Lever's. When he wanted to visit her or take her out, she wouldn't go unless she could bring a friend. On one occasion, he said to me, "Will you do me a big favour? I want to go out with my girl."

"Okay. Sure."

We had to catch a train to Chester and then another from Chester to Birkenhead, as there was no bus service. First we went to his house, and I met his parents. Then it was time for the date. When Walter and I arrived to pick up his girlfriend, Thelma, and her friend, who later would become my wife, Walter introduced us, "Oh, this is Sheila Hurst."

"Oh, how do you do?"

Then we went and sat in the cinema. During the show, I wasn't paying a lot of attention to my partner, though I wasn't ignoring her either. Meanwhile old brother Cross was looking along the aisle to see if I was making any progress, which I wasn't. When we came out, we had to go our separate ways, he with Thelma, and I with Sheila. So that was the start of our friendship. We walked up by Bebington Station to Highcroft and I said, "Cheerio. Shall I see you again—or anything?" She must have answered, "Yes."

I don't think Bud was with us the next time (his thing had gone sour on him for some reason), and I don't remember how I got to Bebington. I must have gone by train, but I'm not sure. But subsequently I bought a bicycle so I could ride from Sealand to Bebington without all the mishmash of going to Chester first and then to Birkenhead. I would cycle the 13 miles each way to meet Sheila, and we'd go to the cinema. The second time, I was almost out of money (that used to happen a lot). I said, "I can pay for one. I can pay for myself. Can you pay for yourself?" I guess she thought it was a bit cheeky, but we managed to pass that over.

On one of our cinema dates, we found ourselves in the middle of an air raid. Things had started to warm up as far as the war was concerned. We had German bombers flying over every evening, about 6:30 p.m.—just as it was getting dark. You could almost set your watch by them. We'd be sitting in the cinema and the warning would flash on the screen. If there was a yellow light, it meant that an air raid was imminent. When the light became red, it meant that the raid was in progress. Sometimes we would sit right through it with the noise echoing all around outside. Then we would come out about 10:30 or 11:00 p.m., and make a mad dash across the road to an old house with a basement they had made into an air shelter. The basement had extra wooden supports and beams across to hold up the floor. There would be half a dozen to 10 or 11 people all huddled together in this so-called air raid shelter, waiting for the raid to pass over. Then Sheila and I would hurry home to Highcroft, about a mile-and-a-half to two miles away.

This got worse as time went on. You could see the fires in Liverpool, which was just across the river. A lot of the bombs actually dropped on Birkenhead, and quite near to Sheila's home. I remember in particular their dining room, which had a very stout dining room table. The family had placed a wire cage underneath, which helped to support the table, and the family used to get under there. I remember that Sheila's sister, Doreen, hated getting under the table. I don't know about the others as I used to buzz right back to camp.

One day, as I was leaving Sheila's, carrying my obligatory tin hat, gas mask and satchel, I suddenly heard ZIT ZIT ZIT ZIT ZIT ah ZIT ZIT. It was shrapnel, falling down from the anti-aircraft shells. The guns were firing up into the air, and chunks of metal were falling down like rain. I went back and sheltered in the porched area of Highcroft where there was an arch I could shelter under. Sheila must have sensed I was there, as she came to the door and said, "You'd better come inside for a little bit until it quiets down."

The same sort of episode was happening back at the base in Sealand. We had bombs dropped on the aerodrome, and there was rumbling and crashing going on at the airfield. On one occasion, I was in the three-storey barrack block when the bombing started. I ran down two sets of stairs and then out. On the base, they had proper air raid shelters sunk in the ground on the airfield and around the barrack blocks. I was about to make a dive for one of these when I looked ahead of me. Here was the back end of a Heinkel German bomber, moving away from me with orange flashes coming from the back. It was the rear gunner, spraying bullets all over the place—and right in my direction. So I hit the floor and then eventually got under a vehicle, which wasn't too smart, as there is gasoline in a vehicle.

I later heard that the Heinkel was shot down near Chester by some Spitfires from a neighbouring station. Some of the crew survived, and I heard that they were arrogant and abusive to the British nurses in the hospital who were caring for them. Then some of the English Air Force guys got out of their hospital beds and were going to pummel them. Fortunately, this German air crew was soon sent elsewhere.

Another time following an air raid warning and after hearing the *All Clear*, I was standing in the doorway when I saw a plane coming over the Welsh mountains. He would turn, bank and turn again. That was an unusual manoeuver for a friendly plane. I didn't want to make a fuss—it would be called a panic maker—but neither did I like what I was seeing. So I dashed down into the annex—a partial air raid shelter—and said, "There's another one up there and I don't like the look of it." The sergeant told me to bring the people down from upstairs, so I dashed along the corridor. BANG! I went down flat. Then I saw the whole front door sail up the stairs, in a huge orange flame. I think the last one was a fire bomb. One had hit the guard room, another hit the sergeant's mess, and the last one hit our building.

When I hit the floor, I had landed on top of another guy, a dental orderly. I thought he might be concussed, so I put my hand on his head and was feeling around. It was all sticky. "Geez!" As I hauled him back towards the annex, we figured out that it was Brylcreem, not blood! But he was definitely concussed—he was out. Unfortunately the bomb hit the guardroom and the sergeant's mess, as well as our place. I don't know how many were injured in the guardroom, but 11 were killed in the sergeant's mess. It wasn't a very nice episode.

On another occasion, Walter Cross and I were on our way back from Bebington. We had caught one train and were crossing town to another station where a train would take us to Sealand—the last train. We ran as fast as we could, but arrived just in time to see the tail lights of the last coach going by the platform. We were stuck. It was about six miles to Sealand, and so we decided to walk. However, when we reached the barrier, the R.A.F. Special Police or S.P.'s, as they were called, insisted that we get in their truck and told us that we would be on charge for being late when we got back to the camp. It was pitch black, of course, so the high military truck drove around Chester picking up all the drunks and throwing them inside.

I started thinking as we drove around and asked Bud, "Say, have you got your Red Cross arm band with you?" We used to carry our arm bands at all times in case we encountered an emergency. He replied, "Yes."

"Well, put it on."

"What for?"

"Never mind. Just put it on."

I was picturing the layout of the camp in my mind. The truck would pull up to a gate where the guard was, and then pull ahead to the guardroom, where they would unload all these airmen. But on the other side of the gate was the section of the camp we were staying in. "Right, Bud," I said. "As soon as it's in the gate, jump."

Sure enough, the truck pulled up to the gate and stopped. Next the guard pulled open the gates. "NOW!" We jumped out before anyone had time to reach the back of the truck. Walking straight across to the other guard I said, "Just going to the other side." We showed our arm bands, and they never knew they had given us a free ride from Chester to Sealand.

On still another occasion, I was returning to Ternhill, the R.A.F. base in Shropshire, Market Drayton, where I had been transferred. As I traveled in the train to Ternhill and looked back towards Liverpool, about 40 miles away, I could see a red glow in the sky. The whole place was ablaze. When I got back to camp, I managed to put a phone call through to Sheila's family at Highcroft in Bebington to see if everybody was okay. They were. I was relieved to hear this because I knew Sheila's Dad used to go fire-watching. The first wave of planes would drop incendiary bombs. They were made of magnesium ribbon, which ignited very rapidly, and this would set buildings on fire so that the bombers behind them could see where to drop their bombs. Think what it must have been like for the fire-watchers, waiting on top of those buildings while this rubbish was coming down—waiting with buckets of sand and shovels to put the fires out!

While I was stationed at Sealand, I got in the black books of a Flight Lieutenant named Dickson. One of our duties was to tidy up the Medical Officer's (M.O.'s) bedroom. I and another guy were busy doing this one day when he said to me, "D'you know, he's got a revolver in that drawer? You're not supposed to have a revolver and neither is he!"

"I don't believe it."

"Have a look."

Just as I was looking, who should walk in but the M.O. himself. We weren't supposed to be looking into other people's drawers, so I apologized. He didn't do much about it either, because he wasn't supposed to have a firearm. Anyway, he was posted to Ternhill first, and then I found myself there again with him. However, we didn't say much to annoy each other.

As part of our exams to get our Leading Aircraftsman, we had to answer all sorts of medical questions. Then we had to go into the operating room where the M.O. would bring out all sorts of instruments, and we had to name each and every one of them. I did my best, and I think I got only one wrong. So he was sort of pleased about that. A short time later, one of the airmen got appendicitis and we had to do something about it, so he asked me for help. So the two of us did the appendectomy in the operating theatre of the camp, and after that we were the best of friends.

There was a pub in Ternhill—a sort of palatial pub out in the country—and when we went there for Christmas drinks, M.O. Dickson treated us—wouldn't let us buy anything. Needless to say, we staggered out of that pub. There was a big airman with me who fell down and rolled into the ditch. I knew I had to somehow get him out of the ditch and back to camp to book him in. I couldn't leave him, or he'd be in trouble and be put on a charge. So I got right down into the ditch, crawled underneath him, pulled his arms over my shoulders, and hauled him like a sack of coal towards the guardroom, with his toes trailing behind on the road. When I reached the guardroom, I just shouted his number and mine (you were given numbers when you booked out), hauled him to the hut, and tossed him on the bed. He never knew a single thing about it—not a single thing.

When I first arrived at Ternhill—I hadn't been there for more than a couple of days—an entire squadron of Polish airmen arrived, 303 Squadron. They'd been flying Hurricanes down on the south coast, and they had been pulled back for a bit of respite. It was September 1940. These airmen were hyper, but who wouldn't be? They drank a lot and had a good time as there was no action in

Ternhill. There was the pub—all decorated with airplanes—located opposite the Ternhill station, but nothing else for miles around. The Polish airmen would get drunk at night and then come into the medical centre the next morning, sick with headaches and so forth. We used to give them a mixture called "Morning After" that we found in the Air Force pharmacopoeia. As I recall, it included ammonia, oil of lemon, nutmeg, and something else that I can't remember. We'd give it to them in a glass and say, "Here, now, drink this down." Either the headache would be gone or they would be violently sick. Either way they were cured.

Another incident happened around Christmas. The doctors had all hiked off to Chester to celebrate, and I was left on duty with an orderly, a member of the Women's Auxiliary Air Force (WAAF). During this time, we had a stray airplane crash on the air field—an Anson, I think it was. The pilot was injured; so we got him out, put him on a stretcher, and took him to the sick bay. We didn't know what was wrong with him, so we left him on the stretcher, which we placed on a bed, head to foot—sort of high up, with a heat lamp over him. I looked at him, gave him some tea, and started to clean him up. He looked as if he'd been shot with little gun pellets. Now I was stuck. I had no medical officer—just one WAAF orderly. The M.O.'s were all whooping it up somewhere, and if I reported this, they'd be in deep trouble, as they had left the station unattended. We were facing a dilemma. So we treated the man for shock, and the WAAF orderly was very good. Eventually the M.O.'s came back. They tended to him and then shipped him off to the hospital. That was a tricky one.

Also around Christmas 1940, I thought Sheila might like to come to Sale and meet my parents. I had been to Highcroft a few times to take her out, and her family all knew me. So when I found out I was going to have a few days' leave, I checked with my Mum. Sheila must have been about 22 at the time, and so was I, yet we still had to ask permission to visit each other's homes. So we took the train to Sale and spent a couple of nice days there with my family.

There was a place in Sale called Lido, quite a big place. In the summer it had a big swimming pool, long and oval. In the winter, they would put a sprung floor over the pool and use it for dances. The tables were slightly higher than the dance floor, and the band would be situated at the top end of the ballroom. There were always two bands, and as one came on or off, the stage would rotate, and the second band would appear. Sheila and I had a really nice time there—a gala time. Later in the War, they turned it into offices. Such a magnificent place to be ruined in that way!

My next posting was to Millom in Cumberland. My friend Bud Cross was also posted there. When we arrived, the camp was in mud. Eeugh! It was only half built, with the airfield unfinished and the huts still under construction. Needless to say there wasn't much to do there, although the Salvation Army did have a canteen in the centre of town where you could go for cookies, coffee and a social time. Come to think of it, the Salvation Army did a lot of work—feeding us and helping us to get to know each other better. One of the M.O.'s at this camp was very nice. We used to sit and talk with him into the evening—just a young guy, who had not long been graduated. Some of the others wouldn't even talk to us—too haughty.

Well Bud had met a girl when we were stationed at Sealand who actually came from Workington, which was not far from Millom. Bud wanted to see her again, but she would agree only if she could bring a friend. So I agreed to go with him. We were sort of sticking together by this time. His girl's parents ran a workingman's club in Workington; so after we had made the round of pubs, we went to her parents' club. They actually lived at the club, and so when we got there, the round of drinks came out again. I was drinking rum, which I hadn't had for a long time. Everyone was saying, "Be happy." But I wasn't happy, I was totally depressed. At one point I went to the bathroom, got a basin full of cold water, and splashed it all over my face. Tried to liven myself up. I wasn't ill—just depressed. I livened up a little, had a few more drinks, and then said we would sleep in the attic, as there was no train back to Millom. It was too late.

So Bud and I went up to the attic for the night. I remember there were two single beds and a lot of junk up there, including a harmonium. I can still see and hear Bud in his underpants, with his glasses sitting at the end of his nose, pumping the harmonium at two o'clock in the morning and singing "Lead kindly light." Hilarious! Then the people down below started to bang, bang, bang on the ceiling, saying, "Go to sleep! Go to sleep!" We had to rise bright and early at about 4:00 a.m. to catch the train from Workington to Millom.

While we were stationed at Millom, I was attached to a place at Silecroft, a few miles north of Millom, with about 50 guys, whom I was to look after. As soon as I got there, they wanted to know what I was going to do about the food. So I told them to leave the matter with me. When I went around on a cookhouse inspection, I found tennis balls in the water tank above the sink, cabbage that was going rotten, and very little food. I could see that something was certainly not right.

On that particular evening, I went and sat by the seawall, where I could look across from Silecroft to the Isle of Mann. There was a coast guard there, as it was a deserted part of the beach where an enemy might land undetected. I used to chat with this guard. On this particular night as I sat with my back to the seawall, I witnessed an airman coming through a gap in the wall and a lady waiting nearby. He was carrying a brown paper parcel, with blood oozing through it. He obviously had meat in the thing. I simply said, "Good evening," and watched as he went off with his wife, presumably to their home.

The next day I telephoned the main camp and said, "Tell me what you are sending to Silecroft, and I'll tell you what we've had to eat for the next four days." They agreed. During the following four days we had next to nothing—dried peas and almost nothing else. I made notes. However, I didn't have to use them, because some of the officers had followed the rations truck in an unmarked car as it left the main camp. They followed the truck to the village where it was unloaded and the food sold. That practice certainly came to a halt in a hurry!

Another time we were called to see a civilian who was absolutely unconscious. We couldn't figure out what was the matter with him. The next morning, he was up and gone. He wasn't an Air Force, guy; he was a civilian. We later learned that there had been a shipwreck and that casks of brandy had been washed up on shore. Obviously he had been into the brandy!

I didn't find out about some of these incidents until I came back from abroad and visited the Tower Ballroom in Blackpool where I got talking with a corporal. He said to me, "Wow. Did you ever create a stir when you were up in Millom!" Then he filled me in about these incidents where they had had to send in the police to make arrests and clear up the problems. Millom was a bit remote—tucked up in the corner of northwest England. I suppose they thought nobody would know what was going on.

Chapter III

It was June 1941 when Bud and I were posted overseas. First we had to assemble at Wilmslow, in Cheshire not far from Sale, where we were kitted out with tropical gear and other necessities. We had been together on the same stations since January 1940, and we didn't want to be split up now if we could avoid it. So when we learned we were on different drafts, we went to see the Adjutant and explained our situation. His response was exceptional for the Forces, but enabled us to stay together.

"Well...Okay. We'll move Bud Cross onto your draft. We'll put him down as Volunteer Cross."

We were soon on our way to Liverpool where we were put on an old tub of a boat called the *Anselm*. It was a Booth Line ship—a really slow steamer—and had been used for Amazon trading before the War. We heard that it had recently returned from the Middle East, and that the crew—probably civilians— had refused return to sea aboard the *Anselm*.

S.S. *Anselm*.

We set off from Liverpool at the tail end of a convoy. Soon
the destroyer came up and asked if we couldn't go a little faster.
We were doing 9 knots flat out—9 knots! Obviously we were too
slow for the convoy, which had to go on without us. So we stopped
at Glasgow to take on more people or assemble more ships. For a
time we were stuck there wondering what was going to happen.
Of course there were all sorts of rumours—that we would be
going ashore, that we would be boarding another ship, etc. People
came and went. However none of these rumours proved to be
true. Instead, we were given a new escort consisting of a destroyer,
a corvette, and the *Challenger*, formerly an Arctic survey vessel,
and off we trundled.

H.M.S. *Challenger*.

We had aircraft coverage with Lockheed Hudsons for about a day and a half, and at three days out, the destroyer had to turn back due to fuel limitations. So we plodded on out into the Atlantic, accompanied only by the corvette and the survey ship. Our ship bobbed up and down a lot, but I managed to avoid being sick. I ate dry bread and apples and stayed midships most of the time, although at intervals, we were required to go to lifeboat stations and other drills.

This routine continued a few more days more before we experienced a bit of a scare. First we saw smoke on the horizon, and then a ship came dashing up. We were relieved to discover that it was one of our own! We were not allowed to break radio silence during the War because that would have told the Germans where we were. The next day somebody saw—or thought they saw—a periscope. Word went around, "Don't panic." Some of the crew were below, asleep in bunks and hammocks, but Bud and I were more fortunate. Our bunks were in the stern. About 5:30 a.m., we experienced a tremendous wallop, followed by an explosion. It was July 4, 1941.

Before the lights dimmed (when the engine stops, the lights go out), I managed to grab my life jacket and race up onto the deck. Sure enough, we had been hit by two torpedoes, and we had over

1400 troops on board. As our ship began to list, the *Challenger* came alongside, but backed off because they knew it would be too dangerous for us to jump from ship to ship.

Funny little incidents come to mind. There was one guy who must have been able to swim out of the hole the torpedo had made in the side of our vessel. I recall him swimming away from us, and the corvette sending a boat after him. As our ship listed more and more, we went to lifeboat stations. However, when they tried to lower the life boats on the high side of the ship, they came crashing down on the men assembled below. There simply were not enough experienced crew to lower the boats properly. Luckily I got into one of the boats being lowered. Once afloat, we drifted towards the *Challenger,* which had positioned itself downwind so that survivors would be carried towards it. The *Challenger* crew hung cat ladders down the sides of their ship—square rope ladders that we could grab and climb up. There were many guys in the water, but a lot more failed to get out of the ship's hold, because the wooden staircases that led to their quarters had been blown away by the explosion, and they had no way out. We tried to lower ropes to haul them out, but there were just too many of them. There was a minister with us—Presbyterian I think—who asked to be lowered into the hold to pray with the men. At first we refused, but he insisted, and so we did as he requested. There is a short write-up about him in the Archives somewhere, but it never made the newspapers because of it being wartime.

As we drifted away from the *Anselm*, we dared not stay too near lest our lifeboat be dragged down with the sinking ship. The sound of singing drifted across the water. There were more than 200 men singing "Abide with Me," which was very tragic. A little while later, as the ship nosed down and the stern rose high out of the water, there was a tremendous noise. I wondered what the heck it was. Somebody had brought a piano on board for a sing-along before we left. The ship was now at 45 degrees. The piano toppled and crashed down along the length of the deck. You can imagine the noise from the strings.

As I reached the deck of the *Challenger*, more and more guys followed until there were 900 of us, some of whom were injured. I remember us all yelling at one soldier who was still in the water, "Come on! Come on! Get up! Get the ladder! Grab the ladder!" When we finally hauled him onto the deck we saw that he was unconscious. Someone said, "Don't bother him. He's had it." I thought, "No way!" So I rolled him onto his stomach, pumped him and gave him Artificial Respiration using the Schafer method, which is to roll him over and press on the back. Suddenly he vomited, got up, and walked away as if nothing had happened. He never looked back.

So there we were in the middle of the Atlantic—off the Azores somewhere—with 1140 men on two small ships. We had lost 278, but we were fortunate not to have lost more. Now we were forced to break radio silence. We called up and they detached a ship called the *Cathay* from another convoy. The *Cathay* was currently employed as a merchant cruiser, but it was really a P&O liner with two guns attached, one fore and one aft. She reached us on July 5, about 24 hours from the time that the torpedo had hit.

Our next ordeal was to transfer from the *Challenger* and corvette to the *Cathay*. Of course, while we were doing it, we were sitting ducks. Fortunately nothing happened. We later found out that the detection gear on the corvette had been on the blink the day we were hit, and that they had had no idea a submarine was below. Once we were hit, of course, they had commenced dropping depth charges.

I remember transferring the injured. Something like a crane was lowered directly over the side of the *Cathay*. Then they hauled the injured on stretchers up onto the *Cathay*, which was high above the deck of the *Challenger*. I recall standing on the derrick arm of the *Challenger*, holding on with one hand, and directing these operations with the other. As it turned out, I was last to leave the *Challenger*. They had a cat ladder over the side of the *Cathay's* hull—a big ship, rising and falling, rising and falling. I had to judge it right and grab onto the ladder, or I would fall between the ships. I could see the guys with the gold epaulets looking over the side, saying, "There's going to be an accident here." I thought, "No. I've got this far. I'm not going to blow this one." So as the ships rose and fell, I waited until l judged the time was right. Then I grabbed it and UP! From my diary, July 5, 1941:

"We gave the *Challenger* and the corvette K20 a big cheer, which was the least we could do for their unstinted generosity and bravery. We find that we have 60–70 injured. Two of our boys are missing, young Jack and a Corporal. Absolutely tuckered out, we get some food and rest. The weather is now fine. My sole possessions are: pyjama trousers, cigarette case, lucky horse shoe, mirror, comb, pay book, fountain pen, identity disc, and £6 in cash. I am rich! Walter turns up in a borrowed naval uniform. We are glad to get this all over."

Pages from Peter's diary 1941.

The *Cathay* was equipped with a proper medical theatre and a place to treat the injured. Of course, there were 1000 guys who needed to be fed. I remember wearing only a pair of pyjama trousers.

Luckily it was warm. It would be another 14 days before we reached Freetown, Sierra Leone, on the west coast of Africa. Convoys from Glasgow could make it this far before having to refuel. Two big rivers flowed out to sea at Freetown, creating a large natural harbour. So it was the preferred stopping place for convoys going around the Cape of Good Hope on their way to the Middle East. The report of the U-boat commander was inaccurate. He claimed that the *Anselm* and the *Challenger* were escorted by three destroyers at the time of the incident. However, according to my diary, there was only one corvette and the *Challenger* escorting the *Anselm*:

> "There were only two escort vessels present at the time of the torpedoing. The *Cathay* reached us 24 hrs. later. Bud and I were assigned night duty and worked in the operating theatre until 1:00 a.m. and were trotting around until 5:30 a.m. We slept on the upper deck under a lifeboat. Two naval officers told us we could not sleep there as it was the Officers' promenade deck. We quickly told them to go and promenade somewhere else.
> July 7: *Challenger* left us.
> A stoker brings us biscuits without fail.
> July 13: full of expectations, hoping to see land. Stay on deck until dark. Straining our eyes for the first glimpse.
> July 14: sighted at 5:00 a.m. Crossed the bar at 7:00 a.m. Some patients transferred to a hospital ship, the *Oxfordshire* (Bibby line), the remainder to a shore hospital."

We didn't know where we were bound. Nobody ever tells you. We knew we were in Number 128 Squadron—it was to be Hurricanes—but whether we were headed for the Far East or elsewhere, we didn't know. Also, there were troops other than Air Force aboard; so they took the remnants of this R.A.F. 128th Squadron and landed us on the shore—about 150 men. I remember the black Africans coming up in their small boats, wanting to sell us things. At the time we thought they all looked the same. Once we had disembarked, we were rigged out in Army uniforms, khaki drill and so on, and also tropical gear, because West Africa—often described as "the white man's grave"—is full of malaria and yellow fever. Once we were kitted out, they put all 150 of us on a little "Puffing Billy" train heading for the tiny village of Bo, 135 miles inland. The journey on this narrow gauge railroad took about 24 hours. They sent us there with a water bowser and one wicker hamper of medical supplies.

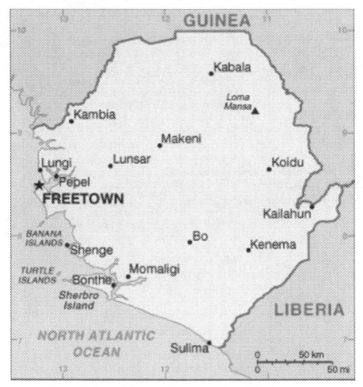

Map of Sierra Leone, West Africa.

When we arrived at Bo, we were greeted by the only four white people in the village: the headmaster of a school, a female school teacher, a governor of some sort, and a medical doctor. The female teacher, an attractive young woman, had come to the platform dressed in a sort of flimsy nightgown pant suit. You can imagine the cat calls and whistles as 150 servicemen poured out of the train. We never again saw her dressed like that. I guess she had come straight from her bed to meet us.

Next we were escorted to a camp just outside the village. It consisted of mud-walled huts with thatched roofs and no windows—just shutters, open to the air. We must have been expected, as mosquito nets had been laid out on each bed. Boy, did we ever need them! The mosquitoes were prolific! We were given a seven-pound box of quinine sulphate powder. Each morning, we had the men line up with their mugs containing some water, into which we would stir a tablespoon of quinine sulphate, and we would watch them while they drank it. Afterwards they were allowed to go on their way. They disliked this routine, as the taste was very bitter, and the quinine sulphate started to cause deafness, but they had to take it to avoid getting malaria. Luckily, we had only one case of malaria, a Christian Scientist, who became very ill. He must somehow have ducked out of the line-up. Otherwise, we did very well with that treatment.

We remained in this camp for three months during which we had to make our own latrines, as well as drainage channels to carry away the rain water from between the huts in order to make the place habitable. Rations were sent to us by train. I call them rations because I wouldn't call them food, and the men were always complaining. One day when they were really angry about the day's rations, they asked me to do something. After warning them not to touch anything, I went straight to the officers' quarters, where the officers were sitting down to eggs and bacon. I spoke to the Adjutant, "The men are complaining about their food." He replied that he would come to see about it after he had finished eating. I said, "No. You had better come NOW!" He did come, and he saw what was supposed to be food for 11 men—one tin of bacon that had been standing in a pan of hot water. Either the Army was sending us their leftovers, or our food was being stolen by someone en route to the camp. Eventually we placed an R.A.F. man with a machine gun on the back of the truck, and the thieving stopped.

Bo, Sierra Leone: main street 1940.

Bo, Sierra Leone: children carrying water 1942.

Bo, Sierra Leone: children carrying fish 1942.

Bo, Sierra Leone: worker spraying oil on standing water to control mosquitoes 1942.

Bo, Sierra Leone: drainage ditch 1942.

Bo, Sierra Leone: native hut under construction.

Bo, Sierra Leone: local ferry.

Bo, Sierra Leone: military quarters 1941.

Bo, Sierra Leone: municipal office and courthouse 1942.

Meanwhile, life at the camp went on. An African boy was assigned to our hut. He made our beds, supplied us with fresh bananas and other fruit, and saw that our laundry was done. The village women did the actual washing down at the river, where they pounded the heck out of our army clothes on the stones. Also the village had a main street and a general store where we could buy pop and chocolate bars, but we were essentially 150 guys with nothing to do. We had a few regular chores, but not many. (There were no airplanes yet, as the airfield was just being built at Hastings, near Freetown.) We were mostly just waiting for additional troops for our squadron, to compensate for the numbers we had lost aboard the *Anselm*.

Soon we began to devise our own entertainment. Somebody started a soccer match with the young African boys from the local school. Could they ever move that ball—in their bare feet! They walked all over us at first, until we started to get the hang of it. Of course, it was very hot—100 degrees Fahrenheit or higher. Bud and I also managed to get some books sent by a church organization in Freetown, one of them about African birds. So we began birdwatching, which occupied our time for awhile. There were so many varieties of birds with glorious colours. We also played chess, using a little set that my father had sent. It consisted of a wallet with black and white pockets into which little chess men, like slivers of plastic, would fit. Bud and I also got many hours of entertainment out of that.

One day, the men organized a cross-country race that would take us around the village, about five miles further on dirt roads, around the village again and back to the camp. I thought I could run reasonably well, and so I entered. I started running with a man called Pym from the south of England who had been a professional runner. We had been running together for awhile when Pym said, "Come on, Pete. Let's go. I'll have to leave you now." Then he took off. I eventually reached the finish line where I collapsed. I was quite proud of my effort, however. I had finished third and received a shaving kit as my prize.

Just outside the village, there was a clinic for Africans run by a doctor from London, England. It was a one-storey building with a quadrangle in the middle. This doctor asked if we would like to help him and we said that we would. He had us sit in the clinic as the Africans came for treatment, and we would write down their various diseases and problems as he explained them. They were suffering from venereal diseases, as well as from yaws and elephantiasis. The Africans would come to us for a couple of weeks and then disappear. We soon learned that they were vacillating between the London doctor and the witch doctor.

The English doctor had a pharmacist, an African who hadn't been on leave for a long time; so he asked if I would look after the pharmacy while he went away for two weeks. I agreed, because during my time at the clinic, I hadn't seen too many people. Well to my surprise, on my first morning in the pharmacy, the place was crammed with people and a steady stream of prescriptions kept coming through the hatch. Dispensing them one at a time, as we were supposed to do, I didn't finish until ten o'clock at night. I said to myself, "This is not going to work." So I looked through the prescriptions to find out which ones were the most common, and made up 80-ounce bottles of those ready for the next day. There was no other way I could cope with the numbers. Meanwhile, the pharmacist who was supposed to be on leave for two weeks ended up being away for a full month!

During the same period the doctor asked me and Bud to help him in the small operating theatre where he did his surgery. We wondered what he did about anaesthetics because there was no anaesthetist. We found out that he gave spinal anaesthetics to patients with problems like hernias and elephantiasis. Elephantiasis is a blockage of the capillaries and prevents the patient from urinating; so the body fills up with fluid. We did surgery for a couple of patients with this disease. When we drained away the excess fluid from one of them, it weighed forty-five pounds.

The villagers of Bo were Mende people. They practised their own religion, which was tied to the seasons. When they had a good harvest or hunting, they would pray to certain gods. They also practised a very strict moral code—much stricter than ours—and they were healthier for it. For example, you couldn't marry anyone from within your own family. Also boys and girls were trained in a secret society until they were mature. We Christians probably thought of them as pagans, but sometimes their beliefs and morals were better than ours. They were pretty nice people and they treated us well. We were strangers in their country, and yet they were friendly and good to us. One of our soldiers, a guy from London in the U.K., was very prejudiced. He would chase the African boys around and try to kick them because he said they were lazy. Indeed, none of them would do anything for him. To Bud and me, however, they were pretty good. They brought us things, and we got along with them just fine.

During this same time, I celebrated my 22nd birthday. (My 21st had been disappointing—running around Connah's Quay in Wales, blowing whistles.) Strangely enough, there was a café in Bo run by an Italian lady. I don't know why she was there. Perhaps her husband worked on the railway. At any rate, she was on her own and she kept a few hens and a little garden. Bud must have said something to her about it being my birthday, and she said,

"Come along and we'll fix something for him." I don't know where she got the food, but we had a really big feed. There was cream cake, jellies, trifle and chicken, and she wouldn't take any money for it. So I celebrated my 22nd birthday in the bush, and it was really good.

You might wonder about the climactic conditions we were facing. It was a hot and steamy jungle. During the wet season—which lasted about six months—the air was filled with the sounds of cockroaches, crickets and other insects. They would start in mid-afternoon and continue in an ever-increasing crescendo throughout the night. Resembling escaping steam, it would start to taper off as the sun rose, but continue until ten or eleven in the morning. Then at half past four in the afternoon, it would start up again. You have to remember that we were at the Equator, where there are exactly twelve hours of daylight and twelve hours of darkness—with variations of less than half an hour. During the wet season, it would rain almost continuously day and night. Then somewhere around October, we would get really violent thunderstorms, following which the clouds would roll away and we wouldn't see rain again until May. It would then get hot and dry eventually, but it would take a long time for the roads and bush to dry out. After about three months we had to leave Bo and go down to Hastings, where they were building the airfield.

Chapter IV

They said they had been building the airfield, but they hadn't done very much to it, and the runway was only six hundred yards long. The Fleet Air Arm were already operating out of this airfield with Fairey Swordfish, Walrus Flying Boats (really old biplanes), and Blackburn Rocks (single-engine planes). On the adjacent river, big amphibious Sunderland Flying Boats could be seen landing and taking off. They were on coastal command and would fly out over the ocean looking for submarines.

My job was to work with the Navy guys whose C.O., in charge of the Air Arm squadron, was a wild man. He used to start drinking at noon, and stay at it for the rest of the day. (Their M.O. wasn't much better.) On one occasion, a six-foot boa constrictor, attracted by the warmth, had wound itself around the engine of an ambulance parked outside the sick quarters. The Africans who discovered it were dancing up and down yelling, "Snake!" Suddenly, this C.O. came out, poked the snake out from beneath the engine, grabbed it by the back of the neck and, holding it at arms' length, strangled it. I'd never seen anything like it!

Another time, Bud and I were walking across the airfield from the Naval side, where we worked, to the R.A.F. side. Suddenly we heard the noise of an aircraft behind us. This was not unusual, but when it got louder, I casually looked around and saw a Walrus, one of the amphibious planes, coming flat out and straight towards us. Of course, we jumped out of the way. The Walrus never left the ground. It went beyond the runway and into the bush where it turned turtle over—landing upside down with its big pusher prop whirling away like an angry dragon.

Bud and I dashed to the plane, knowing there were people inside. As I looked up from underneath, I could see the cockpit panel facing down and gasoline pouring out everywhere. I knew I had to stop it; so I rammed the switches up, and with the ignition off, the engine sputtered and died before it exploded. Then I saw emerging from the plane, first an elbow, then a leg, and finally an arm. Inside were the C.O. and the M.O., along with a terrified air gunner. They had been in the mess, had a few drinks, and gone out to the airfield for a joy ride. When they were told that this plane was grounded, as it had not yet been serviced, they said they were going anyway. They were extremely lucky, as the plane could have gone up like a torch.

Unfortunately, there were others who were not so lucky. When we followed the plane's path from the airfield into the bush, we discovered it had killed two Africans. One of the bodies was sprawled over an ant hill, and as I stooped to examine it, ants began crawling up my legs. As we loaded the bodies into the ambulance, I suddenly felt a lot of pain. I shouted, "Get going! Get going!" When we arrived at the sick quarters, I hastily took off my trousers and splashed rain water over my legs from the 45-gallon drums we had used to collect it. Then I slathered on calamine lotion.

During this time, a lot of our guys came down with malaria— 40 per cent of them. Everybody got it at least once or twice; I got it four or five times. Our base was near an African village, with a swamp in between. The mosquitoes would bite the Africans, then fly over and bite us, at which point we got the parasite and became sick. For when a female mosquito draws blood from an infected person, she passes the parasite to the next person she bites.

You might wonder what we used for diagnosis. I had a book on tropical diseases by Manson and Barr, which I think belonged to the naval doctor. I also had one microscope with an oil immersion lens that wasn't all that good; one three-ounce bottle of geimsa stain (an azo stain that can be used for staining microscope slides); and two microscope slides. Following the procedure of Manson and Barr, I would prick the patient's finger and make a microscope slide with the blood. Then I would stain it and look for parasites. If I found them, I knew this was a case of malaria. I had a bit of a hoo-hah with one of the Medical Officers, who tried to say I had misdiagnosed someone. He was a new man out from England, an Irishman educated in Cardiff. The patient did have malaria, of course.

The principal Medical Officer in Freetown had heard about us, and one day he suddenly paid a visit to see how we were getting on. He was Wing Commander Hackett, an Australian. He found me struggling to do my work with only two slides—which I dared not break—and one bottle of geimsa stain. To make matters worse, we needed distilled water to rinse the slides, and we hadn't been supplied with any. When I asked the Hurricane Flight for some of theirs, I found it to be acidic, as they used it for batteries. So it was no good to us. Finally I resorted to catching my own rain water from the thatched roof. Whenever it rained, I would rush outside, put a bucket under the eaves, catch as much water as I could, then filter it for use with the slides. Years later, when I met Wing Commander Hackett again, he told me he had nearly laughed out loud when he saw what I was doing and how. He had subsequently sent us additional supplies: stains, slides, laboratory equipment, and a trained lab technician from England. I resented the technician's arrival at first, as I had tried so hard to get things going on my own. However, he was very understanding and knew more than I did; so we got along well in the end.

The symptoms for malaria are very typical. First, you shiver; then you're hot; then you shiver again; then you're hot once more. The frontal headache is really enormous—a severe pain right across your forehead. However, you know that it will eventually go away with treatment. I believe they had us on chloroquine, but I'm not sure. I know we had been on quinine sulphate up in the bush, and we were on mepacrine—one of the first anti-malarial drugs developed by Imperial Chemical Industries in Manchester. It is an azo dye mepacrine—a lot easier to take and more palatable than quinine tablets in powder form. The only problem was that everybody's skin turned yellow. It wasn't sunburn—just a pigment in the azo dye. The treatment took about seven days. So you would be in bed for seven days in your hut or billet. Then somebody had the bright idea of sending patients away for a week to the seaside. Eventually this became a "done thing," and a bunch of men would go off to set up tents on the shoreline, including a cookhouse tent. It was quite primitive, but also quite enjoyable. We could swim in the sea, which was easy because the salt water was quite buoyant. However, there were big rollers; so you had to be careful.

During one of my stays, I discovered a little dugout canoe near the shore—just a tree trunk that had been hollowed out. The natives had been using it—probably to fish—and I got their permission to try it. It was quite tippy and had just one paddle. I had paddled out just a little way when it tipped over and dumped me into the water. At first I held onto the paddle and headed to shore, but when I realized the boat was still out there, I swam back and brought it in.

Sierra Leone: Peter (back) and friend with dugout canoes at the seashore.

The last person to arrive at camp would be assigned to the cookhouse doing heavy jobs like carrying pails or dishes full of water to prepare the meal. The sweat would pour out of you, and it was very tempting to remove your shirt. I don't remember whether I removed my shirt or not, but I did get sunstroke while on cookhouse duty. Lying on my cot feeling really sick, I knew what was wrong and that I needed to get back to the base for assistance.

When I asked for someone to accompany me, not one of my companions agreed. So I set off on my own. I circumnavigated each native village, going from behind one tree to the next, until I reached the main road. It was dark—pitch black—and I had seven miles to go. Eventually I reached the guard house of an army camp, where an African sentry was on duty. He had what I would call an itchy finger. He shouted, "Halt! Who goes there?" I replied, "Friend," but it didn't make any impression on him. He yelled "Halt!" over and over again. Finally, I shouted, "Bring your officer! Bring your officer!" He continued to shout, "Halt." Finally something must have sunk in. The next thing I remember is sitting in the guard room of this camp with a Corporal—a European—but I don't remember anything after that.

I awoke in a hospital in Freetown with several people bending over me. When they realized that I was suffering from sunstroke, they did what was necessary to lower my temperature. There was a minor problem, however. When you get sunstroke, it's considered to be your own fault, and you can be put on the charge. That means you could be put in the jug or made to do chores—things like that. Fortunately I still had the balance of a few days of my leave left—my seven-day leave. So I pretended to be better before the seven days were up so that I would not be considered AWOL.

Meanwhile, the food we were getting at the camp had been going steadily downhill. Originally, we were fed by the Navy, who had ships with access to good food. However, the army was now supplying us from another camp some distance away. I think they were giving us their leftovers. It was pretty awful. The food was brought in Crossley trucks—huge, high vehicles, open at the top, with large, high wheels. One day the driver happened to look in the mirror as he was passing the native village, and he saw the native helpers at the back of the truck tossing food overboard to their friends below. No wonder we had been short! On the next trip, we posted an Air Force guy with a Tommy gun to the back of the truck to make sure it didn't happen again.

We had one other incident with the local villagers. An R.A.F. man came to me in the lab one day and asked, "Are you using methanol?" I replied that I was. He wanted to know how much. I said, "Not much. Do you see that bottle you gave me? There's hardly anything out of it." Eventually we figured out what had happened. The methanol was used as a solvent on the wings of the airplanes. It was stored in 45-gallon drums, which were kept in the compound. Well, some of the villagers worked in the compound doing manual labour; and they had been stealing the methanol. I remembered one of them saying, "Oh, big dance in the village tonight. You come! Big dance. Lots of gin." I realized they'd been stealing the methanol, rolling the big drums down the riverbank, floating them across the river by boat, rolling them up the other side, and having a whale of a time drinking it. And it can be deadly. So we put a native guard on duty, but that didn't work because he was beaten up. So two or three R.A.F. guys with Thompson guns were put on guard. They fired their guns without hitting anybody, and that was the end of it.

At one point I was put on anti-malaria patrol. Once a week, I had to visit the native village, spray the huts, and put oil on any stagnant water. I would be accompanied by 12 African men equipped with spray guns. I would go to each house and ask permission to come in and spray. It wasn't very effective, but we had to do it. I used to go ahead and negotiate with whoever was in the next house—in a village of 50 or so houses. I had to be very tactful, and it wasn't easy to ask, "Can the boys come in and spray?" when they might be preparing a meal or doing something else of importance.

There was one African man in the spray gang who thought he should be in charge. Originally from Freetown, he thought he was above the rest. When he came late one day, I said, "You are supposed to be on time, you know. You'll have to come early tomorrow." The next day he came late again. "If you come late again, you'll lose a day's pay." When he was late again the following day, I said, "Go home. You won't get pay for today. Come early tomorrow, but go home now. No point in you staying." Of course the others were watching this battle of wits. He tagged along for awhile, but I repeated, "Go home. You won't get any pay for today." Eventually, at about 11:00 a.m., he left. I had to make sure he did; otherwise I would have had no control of the men. They had to know who was in charge.

As we went around the village, we came to a stockade—about seven feet high with spikes at the top and encircling many hundred yards. I wondered what it was; so I walked over and opened the door a crack to see what was inside. All I could see was a lot of African women preparing food. When they saw me, they began yelling and screaming. I had stumbled into their secret society—for women only—called *bundu*. I'd heard about it before. At a certain age, girls go into *bundu* and boys go into *poro*. The girls learn about housekeeping and other matters that women need to know. The boys are taught to hunt and fish—all the things a man has to know. They come out with marks on their cheekbones—made, I think, with hot stones—and also marks on their arms. Anyway, I had stumbled into *bundu*—an absolute no-no for any man, black or white. So the screaming went on. I pulled the door behind me and stood with my back to the stockade. All the male villagers came running. My head boy spoke French, and he asked me in French what I had done. Surrounded by about 50 male Africans, I had to think my way out of this. So I said, "Sorry, I did go into *bundu*. But there's nothing over the gate that says this IS *bundu*. I know what *bundu* is." I made my point, and for a few minutes, they gabbled together. All of a sudden they started to laugh, and one of them asked, "You want a nice girl when she comes out of *bundu?*" They had turned it into a joke, but it had been a little tricky for awhile.

During the same period as I went from house to house in the village, one of the Africans brought out a bicycle and offered it to me for a ride. I realized that they wanted to see if I COULD ride it. So I mounted the bike and rode up the narrow footpath, turning around at the end and riding back again. Next I took my hands off the handlebars and put them in my pockets—no hands. They went screaming mad at this because when they rode the bike themselves, they would grip the handle bars tightly.

The most serious incident I recall from those days involved an outbreak of yellow fever. It wasn't in our village, but in a village half way to Freetown. There was an army camp nearby, and one soldier had actually died of yellow fever; so there was a big panic, although we all had had yellow fever injections before leaving the U.K. This disease affects your liver, turning your body, including your eyes, yellow. It's often fatal, and is carried by one particular mosquito called *Aedes aegypti*. This mosquito has a unique appearance—it looks like it's wearing a black-and-white rugby jersey. But where was it coming from? That was the question. So I was assigned to find the source.

They dropped me off in the affected village with my African crew, whereas everybody else had to drive through quickly. I knew that mosquitoes breed in standing water, but I didn't see any water, until I looked around at the back of the huts where they threw empty bottles and food cans out their windows. Sure enough, these containers were half full of water left over from the rainy season. Mosquitoes were breeding in them because the rest of the area had dried up. Just as I was about to return to camp to report this situation, a whole retinue of civilians arrived from Freetown. They asked, "What are you doing here? Who are you?"

"I was sent to find the source of the yellow fever."

"Who sent you?"

"My M.O."

"What have you found and what do you need?"

"Two or three trucks to collect all this garbage and cart it away."

"Okay, okay, we'll fix it."

And that was the end of that. Nobody else had really bothered.

I believe my M.O. had given me the assignment just to get rid of me. He wanted me gone, though I don't know why. True, he was a bully and wouldn't listen. Maybe it was because I'd been out there longer and been to Bo, away from Freetown. Also, I had worked with the civilian doctor in his clinic. He, on the other hand, had come straight from the U.K. He may have resented the fact that I knew what I was talking about.

On one occasion, I was driving an ambulance back to camp with 12 African men in the back when this same M.O. stopped us and started to harangue me in front of my men—accusing me of wasting time in Freetown and the African village instead of doing my job of spraying. By this time I had had just about enough. He was standing in front of me; so I said, "Get out of my way," calling him by his surname. "There's no one here but you and I, and these 12 guys are on my side. I'll run you down." When I started the engine and drove towards him, he jumped out of the way. Then I said to him, "Nobody else needs to know about this." I never heard anything from him after that.

Some time later, a Wellington bomber arrived at our airport, Hastings, as we called it by then. The bomber's last stop had been Gibraltar. During the landing, it was absolutely sheeting down with rain, and I don't know how the pilot could see anything. When he managed to land safely on our short runway, everyone cheered. After all, a Wellington bomber is not a small plane, and it carries a crew of about five. The crew went off to the mess to eat, with plans to depart the next day. In the morning they refuelled and prepared to take off. As I have mentioned, our runway was only 600 yards long, with a mountain at one end and a swamp at the other. The usual technique was to put your back to the mountain and give it the gun. Unfortunately, when the pilot reached the end of the runway and tried to float it off by snatching the wheels up, the plane failed to make it, crashing instead and bursting into flames. We rushed to the site, managing to rescue all the crew and get them into the sick bay where we did what we could, but we were not equipped to treat burns. Our Welsh M.O. made the decision to send them to Freetown for treatment. Unfortunately they were sent to the Army hospital, which had no experience with burns. There they attempted to scrub the burns clean, and the poor burn victims died. Our M.O. should have contacted Wing Commander Hackett, the principal R.A.F. medical officer in Freetown, who would have supervised the treatment. As a result, the M.O. got his just desserts. They shipped him off to Kano, at the base of the Sahara Desert, much to our relief.

At one point during my stay in Sierra Leone, the R.A.F. began advertising for people to become parachute jumping instructors. They had a training centre in England, and so I applied. Word came back that I had to pass a medical, which turned out to be a really tough one. The most difficult part was holding up a column of mercury by blowing into the column. I managed to get through it, however. Then word came back that I had to have 200 hours of flying experience—not as a pilot, but as air crew. So I began to beg rides whenever a plane was going up and I was off duty. My very first flight was a meteorological one which occurred each morning at seven o'clock—in a Fairey Swordfish, a Fleet Air Arm biplane with an open cockpit, piloted by Wing Commander Gibbs, who was about 43 years old. I sat at the back in the gunner's seat. I had a parachute that I was supposed to clip on my harness at the front. However, I found it to be a nuisance, so I placed it in the stowing rack. The ground temperature was 73° F, and I was to take the temperature every 1000 feet. We went up to 14,000 feet just as the sun was coming up—really quite a sight. It was 32°F by now, and we could see a skin of ice forming on the wings. Commander Gibbs said we couldn't go higher because the air was becoming rarified. As we descended my eardrums hurt something awful, but I knew we had to come down sooner or later; so I crouched in the cockpit as we came down, and afterwards the Navy M.O. syringed my ears out. Apparently there was a buildup of wax that was adding to the pressure on my eardrums.

Another time I flew in a Blackburn Rock, much like a Hurricane, with a seat in the back. We went up the French Guinea Coast because the colony next to us belonged to the French, and France and her territories were now under German control. Our task was to fly up the coast so that the men responsible for our radar could test its effectiveness as we returned. On one flight I could see orange flashes and the pilot said that either the Germans or the French were taking pot shots at us with their anti-aircraft guns.

I took as many flights as I could and logged the miles and my time in the air. One time I caught a ride on a R.A.F. Lockheed Hudson, a twin-engine coastal command plane that would go out looking for German submarines. This plane was equipped with two depth charges under the wings, forward firing guns, and a rear gunner. Pointing to a Thompson gun, one of the crew asked me if I knew how to use it. There was a little window on the side of the plane, and you would put the gun on a peg. The gun has a round pan of bullets mounted above the muzzle. "If we have any problems, you've got to use it," he said, "But don't shoot the tail off our plane."

In regular gun turrets, there is a cut-off point; otherwise, you could hit the tail, but in my position, there was no such limitation. Our takeoff was rather interesting. This was a Lockheed with a nose wheel at the front like many planes of today. I think they used it because we had such a short runway. There was also the weight of the turret in the back. Just before takeoff, everyone moved to the front of the plane and stood behind the pilot and navigator. Then the pilot gave it everything it had.

We were out most of the day—down the coast of Liberia looking for ships trying to sneak by, and eventually down the coast of South Africa. We didn't see much, although there were some strange merchant ships off the Liberian coast, which we reported. Finally, the pilot asked, "Shall we take another look?" "No, we haven't got enough fuel," replied the navigator. When we arrived back at the airfield, it was almost dusk, and the flares were out so that we could see the runway. I don't think there was a teacup of gasoline to spare at the end of our flight.

I experienced another exciting flight on New Year's Day. I was sure the air gunner (A.G.) would not want to go up following New Year's Eve, so I offered to go in his place. When I arrived at the hangar, the maintenance crew said, "You're not going up with *him*, are you?" They were referring to a young sub-lieutenant pilot with the Fleet Air Arm, who had been out drinking until 3:00 a.m. with some nurses from Freetown hospital. He eventually emerged through the fog, dragging his parachute behind him. I said, "Doesn't look good, does it?" "Oh well, we'll just go up and make a noise," he replied. We taxied along the runway, and as soon as the wheels were up, he put it hard over, as if he were leaving an aircraft carrier. I saw the huts spinning around the wing tips; and thought to myself that it was a good start. As we levelled off and started to climb, I took readings every 1000 feet. At 8000 feet, he yelled down the speaking tube, which was something like a vacuum cleaner tube, "Have you got all the readings yet?"

"No, not yet."

Eventually, I called back, "Yes, I've got them all now."

He put the nose down and hauled back on the stick, and I thought, "He's going to LOOP this thing, and I'm not even strapped in! Can't even reach the chute—it's in the stow rack." I grabbed a support inside the cockpit and then he performed what is called a stalled turn, rolling it out on the top of the loop, and then straight out of that, a second one. I managed to catch my breath and yell down the tube, "What the H__ do you think you are doing?"

"Weren't you strapped in?"

"NO, I WAS NOT!"

"Oh, God!"

It just so happens that the Fairey Swordfish is a plane with an open cockpit. What had he been doing? Showing off to the nurses he had been drinking with the night before. In the end, nothing ever came of my application to be a parachuting instructor. The need for these instructors had fallen off, whereas there were very few recruits who wanted to go into the medical branch of the R.A.F because of the low pay. So I just stayed put.

Meanwhile, I had always been interested in boats and sailing. So when a naval orderly and I obtained a wing tip float from a Walrus sea plane, we made a sailboat out of it that was big enough to seat two. So early one morning, we set out for Freetown on the big river that flows out there. We must have been crazy, as it was 13 or 14 miles away, and we would have to paddle back again. At any rate, we did go and when we saw the evening plane coming in, we knew it was time to paddle back. Well no sooner had we started back, than the naval guy dropped his paddle over the side. This left us with only one paddle, and there was nowhere to land.

We thought of tying up for the night, but with only a short rope and the river being tidal, we risked being pulled under. We had no choice but to paddle furiously with our one paddle. There was a native dhow just ahead of us, and we yelled and yelled at them, but they took no notice at first. Finally they slowed and let us catch up. There was an albino on board who seemed to be in charge; the rest of the crew were black. I felt that we would be much safer on their dhow than on our little aluminum boat made from a seaplane float. So we tied our little boat behind. However, they were disinclined to go to Hastings, the nearest point to our airfield. Instead they landed at a little village on the shoreline way past where we wanted to be. When we disembarked and kicked the sand, it was phosphorescent, which was quite interesting.

We soon realized we had a problem. None of the villagers were Mendi or Temni, and although I knew a few words of the latter, I had no idea what they were talking about. I soon discovered as well that they knew no English. However, I pulled a small diary from my pocket with a pencil on one end, and I drew a little map of the river showing where the airfield was. I indicated that that was where we wanted to go, and they got the message. So they gave us a native boy as a guide through the swamps back to the main road which led to the airfield, though it was quite a long way. We also communicated that if they would bring our boat back, we would make a big *dash*, which means payment. Eventually we got back to the main road and to our camp. The next morning, we were told that somebody wanted us outside. Twelve Africans from the little village had arrived with our boat, all of them with hands out, waiting to be paid. We paid them willingly.

What else can I tell you about Hastings? We were Number 128 Air Squadron, and when we first arrived, we had no planes. Eventually they did send us three Hurricanes in packing cases. They were offloaded from a ship in Freetown, then floated up the river on barges to the point nearest our airfield—about 13 miles away. How were we to get them from the river to the airfield? We rounded up a bunch of men, put logs under the crates, and rolled them up from the river bank. We used two planes for active service and kept the third for spare parts. We made the packing cases into an office and a sick bay. Once these planes were serviceable, we had no further trouble from the Free French, who had been flying over Freetown, taking photographs of the convoys and giving them to the Germans. We subsequently shot down two of them.

We occasionally went to Freetown and to the local shops where we could buy a few things. There were also a few street vendors. However, the dealers were mostly Lebanese, Syrians or Asians. Apparently they had at one time cornered all the salt, which the Africans needed for their cooking, and were charging the earth for it—a pretty miserable thing to do. On one trip to Freetown, I had a photograph taken—quite an amusing experience. An African man owned a shop where he could take photographs. When I arrived at his establishment, he took me through the shop into the back garden where he had a greenhouse. I sat at one end, and he and the camera were at the other end, producing a kind of diffused lighting. First he positioned me on a piano stool and said, "Smile." Then he whipped the lens cap off his camera, waved it around in his hand while he counted to three. Then he popped it right back on. That was the exposure. The emulsion on the film was really slow, but the photograph came out alright. I guess he did a small business that way, taking photographs of people who were stationed in Freetown during the War.

Sierra Leone: Peter and R.A.F. friends on a trip to Freetown 1942.

**Freetown, Sierra Leone: photograph of Peter
taken by African photographer 1942.**

Sierra Leone: Peter on the airfield at Hastings 1942.

Sierra Leone: Peter in his sailboat made from the wingtip float of a Walrus seaplane 1942.

Planes flown out of Hastings airfield, Sierra Leone: Lockheed Hudson.

**Planes flown out of Hastings airfield,
Sierra Leone: Fairey Swordfish.**

**Planes flown out of Hastings airfield,
Sierra Leone: Walrus (recovery by U.K. Cruiser).**

Most of our time, however, was spent at the base where we made our own amusements. Once we were entertained by a troupe of 24 who had arrived by boat at Freetown where they heard about us. In the hangar we had a lot of 45-gallon oil drums, planks and blankets; so we made a stage for them to perform on. A group of English contractors wanted to come as guests of the C.O. and asked us to reserve the first four rows for them, but they had treated us badly in Freetown, driving past us in a cloud of dust and never offering us a ride. So when they appeared at the back of the hangar, 400 men stood up and booed them out of the building; so they never even got to see the show.

Finally, I must tell you about my 23rd birthday celebration. In Sierra Leone, we were allowed two bottles of beer a week. So Bud and I had saved up our bottles for my birthday. The beer we obtained was from Canada. One was called Canada Bud and was 9% alcohol. The other was called White Chief and was 12-½ %—pretty heavy compared to the 2% English beer we were used to. We invited a few friends to join us, warning them about the strength of the beer. Nevertheless, by about 8:00 o'clock they were drunk. We couldn't let them walk home, because they might lose their way and get bitten to death by mosquitoes. So we piled them all into the ambulance and drove around to their various huts where we would open the door, push the guy in, and shut the door behind him. Fortunately Bud and I, who knew what the beer was like, had remained sober.

Chapter V

Life at Hastings Air Force Base in Sierra Leone continued until one day it was time to go home. Bud Cross had returned to England early because of eye trouble. He had had measles as a child, and the bright African sunlight had seemed to make his problem worse. I was sorry to see him leave because after sticking together so long and through so many trials and tribulations, we had hoped to return home together. That, however, was not to be. Bud returned to England ahead of me and was posted to a station in the Midlands.

When my turn came, I was to travel aboard the *Cuba*, a French liner captured in Australia near the beginning of the War and subsequently used as a troop ship. I travelled to Freetown and boarded this ship with 11 other R.A.F. men. Surprisingly the ship appeared almost empty; there didn't seem to be anyone else aboard apart from the crew. I guess the ship and its crew had completed their mission and were also heading home. My only concern was that the *Cuba* would be travelling unescorted. After my experiences aboard the *Anselm*, I wasn't very happy about that. Unwilling to go below, I slept on the hard teak deck for the entire voyage—all the way from Freetown to Glasgow. Fortunately the ship was fairly fast, doing about 20 knots—quite good for those days and faster than a submarine. Of course, if a submarine were ahead of you, he'd still have you as a target. We did spot several flares—possibly signs of a German submarine—but barrelled straight on to Glasgow without incident, arriving safely on December 2, 1942.

It felt really cold that day as the twelve of us hurried ashore in search of decent food. Of course, we had just come from the tropics. We entered a café, and they must have sensed what our situation was, for they brought us all sorts of food including Scotch broth. Sitting at the table, I picked up a piece of bread and found myself holding it up to the light in search of weevils. I had done this for two years abroad, and it had become an automatic reaction: *pick up your bread and get the weevils out.*

Next they moved us down to Blackpool, a recruiting area where there were lots of accommodations such as boarding houses. There we were required to go on parade each morning. The first morning we had to line up in the freezing December weather with all the new recruits. We waited and waited as all the others were dismissed in their turn, standing to the last because no one knew what to do with us. On the second day I went to the Warrant Officer and advised him that as we had just returned from the tropics, we were being frozen stiff on the parade ground. I informed him where we were staying and said, "If you want us, phone." There was no way we would continue to stand in the cold.

When we got our first leave, I went home to Manchester to visit my parents. Then I headed down to London to see Sheila, who by this time had joined the Armed Forces. I cannot recall whether or not I also went to Bebington to visit her parents. Following my two-week leave, I was posted to Sealand, near Chester, where I had been stationed prior to going abroad. I had asked for this posting because it was close to Manchester and not far from Bebington. When I arrived at Sealand, I was surprised to see some of the same men who had been there before I went away. When they asked me about all that had happened, I tried to tell them little bits of stuff without being too dramatic. However, they weren't very interested or friendly. They had never been abroad—

in fact they had never been anywhere at all, and they seemed to resent the fact that I had. Some of these men had been promoted to the rank of Corporal even though they had joined up long after me, and this fact didn't help. When we went to our lunch room—which was attached to the sick quarters—their language and topics of conversation embarrassed me. When they saw my reaction, they piled it on even more. You have to understand that before I went to Sierra Leone, there had been few women in the forces. When I returned there were lots. Not only that, but we had been without the company of women for a long time. So I was uncomfortable.

Sheila Hurst 1941.

In the sick quarters I became reacquainted with a WAAF named Eileen Dahl, who had been there before I went abroad. She was Danish and had escaped from Denmark with her parents. She and I had much to talk about, including music. Unbeknown to me, she was dating the Medical Officer of the unit. So I started to get all sorts of attachments to other locations (they were "attachments," not postings, as only the Air Ministry could do a real posting); not only that but the M.O. accused me of smoking in the sick bay; and the Flight Sergeant began to look for every opportunity to give me a hard time. At first I wondered what it was all about, but learned much later that the M.O. was unhappy because I was friendly with his girl. Eileen was eventually sent to Air Force hospital for what was conveniently called an "abdominal adhesion," the M.O. presumably being the culprit.

On one of these "attachments," I was sent to a village in South Wales, not far from Swansea where I was billeted with a Welsh family. They had one child, a girl about eight years old. The family spoke only Welsh to one another, although the parents would address me in English. The daughter, however, never did. One day I saw her playing with a group of child evacuees from London, and to my surprise, I heard her chattering away to them in English. Each morning as I walked from my billet down to the camp, I would see people in the houses across the road peeking out from behind their curtains. On the second day in this "land of the waving curtains," I waved back. Although they didn't know what to do, they tentatively waved back, and I let them know that I had seen them. It wasn't long, however, before I was sent back to Sealand.

My next attachment was to Welford Park in Newbury, Berkshire, west of Reading. I had received my warrant and everything else that was needed, and since I had been to Sealand before and knew my way around, it occurred to me that if I could get off a day early, I could go to London on the way and visit Sheila. So I got my pass, sorted everything out and boarded a train for London. Fortunately I had left a telephone number with one of the men in sick quarters, for the next morning, I received a frantic phone call from him. "Come back at once to Sealand.

Your posting has been cancelled." I caught the first train back and arrived at about three in the afternoon. When I reported in, I was informed by the sergeant in charge (appropriately named "Sergeant Death") that I would be placed on a charge.

"What for?"

"For not reporting for duty at 0.800 hours."

I knew as well that, because I had already used the railway warrant, I would also be charged with "misappropriation of Air Force funds." I had to think my way out of this one. My biggest problem was the railway warrant, which I had in fact used. Then it occurred to me that the warrant was probably still at the little platformed station about six miles out of Chester where I had used it. So I returned there and asked the Station Master if he still had the warrant. When I knew that he did still have it, I offered to pay the single fare from Sealand to Welford Park in return for the warrant. He agreed. So I went to the orderly room at the camp and returned the warrant. That was one problem solved. Now I had to tackle Sergeant Death.

Death had often boasted in the staff room that if you knew the *King's Regulations* well enough, you could get out of almost anything. So I decided to put him to the test. The *King's Regulations* was like a big Bible, presumably started many years ago for army personnel. It contained all sorts of regulations about what you could and could not do, and there was usually some little clause that would provide a loophole. In fact, I didn't even need to look my situation up. I said to the sergeant, "Oh, the charge that you have just posted in the guard room, I think you had better cancel it."

"What do you mean?"

"I think you had better cancel it because it isn't valid."

"What do you mean, it isn't valid?"

"You have often boasted that if you knew *King's Regulations* well enough you could get out of anything."

"Yes."

"Well, you didn't report me as being absent from duty at 0.800 hours; you waited until three o'clock in the afternoon before you reported me. So go to the guard room and cancel it because it won't stick."

So that was how I got out of that situation.

Next I was sent to a station in York where they pulled in crashed aircraft and disassembled them. It wasn't a base—just a big yard—and everyone lived out in private billets with Air Force paying for food and accommodations. I found accommodation with an older woman. I believe either she or her husband had served in the First World War. I was given a little bedroom which obviously had been occupied before by a girl. When I inquired, my landlady told me that her niece, now in the Air Force and posted at Sealand, had previously occupied the room. As I examined the books on the shelves, I could see that the niece was a good reader. There was an interesting selection, including Lawrence of Arabia's *Seven Pillars of Wisdom.* Things went well enough at York, where I had about 50 people to look after.

In the meantime, Sheila was still posted in London, and things seemed to be cooling off a bit with her—perhaps because she was now more exposed to the "wicked world." Anyway, on one occasion, a young WAAF came into the sick bay for a minor treatment. When we started chatting, she told me there was a dance that night at the local village and asked if I would like to go. I said, "Sure." When I arrived, however, she was dancing with somebody else. Eventually I did get to dance with her, and the next morning back at the camp, I was told that I was in big trouble. I asked, "What do you mean, I'm in trouble?"

"You were dancing last night with the Staff Sergeant of Police's girlfriend."

The Staff Sergeant in question was a big, burly guy with red hair and a temper to match, and I knew that he could come down pretty heavily on me if I wanted to get in and out of camp. So I decided to face up to him and apologize at my earliest opportunity. When I did manage to speak to him, I said, "Look, I'm sorry. I didn't realize she was your girlfriend." To my surprise, he replied, "That's all right. Never mind. You go ahead." Eventually the girl started hanging onto me and getting really serious. One day she told me she was bringing her mother down to meet me. The day her mother was to arrive, I went for a long bicycle ride. I had been out for quite awhile and was returning home when, as I rounded a corner, there they were waiting at the bus stop. My bicycle suddenly reared up like a stallion and headed in the opposite direction. I had avoided that situation by the skin of my teeth.

Meanwhile my landlady's daughter was about to get married, and her niece, stationed at Sealand, was unable to get leave for the wedding. So I said, "I'll see what I can do." I wrote a letter to the WAAF officer in Sealand, with whom I had some acquaintance, saying that this girl had lived with my landlady for years and was like one of the family. Could she not get some time off for the wedding? I was thinking, perhaps, of one or two days. Well, to my astonishment, she was granted four days! After that, I couldn't do anything wrong in that household.

The wedding went well, with some relatives visiting from Yorkshire. I couldn't understand a word they said. Whether they were just putting it on for my benefit, I never knew, but their dialect was one I had never heard before, and I'd been around a bit. The niece—a nice looking girl with golden hair and blue eyes—stayed for her four days. When I asked if she would like to see a play in York, she agreed to go. We enjoyed a very nice evening, but unfortunately she was already engaged to a Polish airman. It was a nice interlude, nonetheless.

It wasn't long before I found myself posted back to Sealand, where I had a few more adventures. On one occasion, I had to take a psychiatric patient, an airman, to Wilmslow. The patient and I were in the back of the ambulance, and there were two drivers—both WAAFs. On our way back to Sealand, I asked if we could stop at my parents' house in Sale where I had some records and we could cook up some food. They agreed, and while I was playing the records and the two WAAFs were cooking in the kitchen, who should walk in but my father. Why he had come home in the middle of the day I cannot remember, but he walked in and accepted the situation with a certain amount of aplomb. So after eating our food, we headed back to Sealand, where I got into big trouble for taking so long to deliver the patient.

However, I did get to know one of the WAAF drivers, who subsequently invited me to visit her home, since she had visited mine. She lived in Heswell on the Wirral, and her father must have been in a fairly big business in Liverpool because they had a beautiful home. I didn't have a vehicle in those days, so I took the bus. I walked up the long drive to her home, where she met me at the door dressed very nicely in civilian clothes. (Up to this point I had only seen her in her uniform.) She ushered me into the dining room, which was all set out with silverware (real silverware, none of your K-mart stuff). We enjoyed a nice visit, and afterwards she and I went to the cinema a few times. I eventually learned that there was already a man in her life—probably in the Merchant Navy—and that he was coming back. So that was the end of that little episode.

Following this, I received word that I was to go to Halton, about 40 miles from London, to the Institute of Pathology and Tropical Medicine. The Wing Commander at Halton was none other than Wing Commander Hackett, whom I had known in West Africa. I think it was at his instigation that I was sent there. Off I went to shake the ashes of Sealand from my boots, and I wasn't a bit sorry.

I was sent on a six-month course in the Chiltern Hills on tropical diseases, tropical medicine and general lab work. We did blood counts, plasma estimations, blood sugars and other bacteriological tests. People came in with diphtheria and infected throats, as well as many other ailments. It was a very good course, designed to train us to go into hospital labs on any station that we happened to be sent to. I learned a great deal, and the weather became a little milder. During that time, I got my first kidney stone. I was doubled over with pain, and two of my companions gave me a fireman's chair lift over to sick quarters. When we arrived, the corporal in charge of the sick bay was shaving, and the M.O. was having breakfast. I was really in agony. When the young M.O. finally arrived, he said, "Oh yes, appendicitis."

"You silly so-and-so, it's on the wrong side!"

I wasn't at all polite. I swore at him, and the next thing I remember was waking up in a bed in one of the wards. My two buddies were there, and sitting at the end of my bed was Wing Commander Hackett, with gold braid on his arms. The guys must have wondered who I was that a Wing Commander had come to see me. The next day the Corporal and the M.O. were sent to far away places.

After Halton, I had only one more attachment—at Enstone, near Oxford where there was a night flying school. Using Wellington Bombers that had been withdrawn from operations, they were training pilots for night bombing raids over Germany or elsewhere on the Continent. These Wellingtons were very sturdy planes once they were up, but getting them up could be a problem because they were underpowered with two radial engines, and of course, they carried a heavy load. These planes frequently crashed on landing or take-off, and I recall one week when I didn't get to bed at all as there was a crash every night. Our job was to go out to the site, get the men out and then take them by ambulance to Oxford, as we didn't have facilities at our airfield to handle major injuries.

During my time at Enstone, I witnessed a crash in one of the nearby fields. I had previously purchased an Ordnance Survey (O.S.) map of the local area and had it pinned on the wall so that when there was a crash, I would know exactly where it would be. When the call came to say there had been a crash, I asked which way the ambulance had gone. When I heard the direction it had taken, I knew they wouldn't be able to get to the site, as there was a river in the way. There was a spare ambulance in the sick quarters; so I jumped into it and got the WAAF driver to come with me. It was dark, and we could see flames. When we reached the crash site, we could see men scattered in the field. It was not very pleasant. The plane was blazing like "one o'clock" and ammunition was going off, like fireworks, all over the place. It was really dangerous. To make matters worse, the WAAF driver wasn't medically trained in any way, shape or form, but she helped me as best she could. We found some of the men and put them into our small ambulance. The other ambulance would not arrive until about 20 minutes later. We took some of these men to the hospital in Oxford, but one man, a New Zealander, died on the way. When we reached the hospital, they said we had to take the dead man back to Enstone. At this point, I had just about had enough. We had no morgue at Enstone, so I asked, "Do you not have a morgue here? Then keep him here, and we will send for him in the morning." I also said, "I don't know WHO you are or WHAT you are, but that's the way it's going to be." Then to the trembling R.A.F driver, I said, "Start your engine; we're leaving." When I reported for work the next day, my M.O. suggested I that I take a leave; so I took a weekend pass. In the end, they played "hell" with me for going to the crash site, and my WAAF driver received absolutely no recognition. We had done what we could. In a way, they were correct, but we couldn't just sit there and do nothing.

There is a little sequel to this story. One of the airmen involved in the crash had left behind a flying jacket—one with a button-up collar. These jackets were much sought after because the wearer didn't need to put on a collar and tie. With just the jacket, he would appear properly dressed. Normally, the belongings of injured people would remain in my custody. So when word came down through my M.O. that the Commanding Officer (C.O.) of my station wanted the jacket, I agreed to give it to him if he would sign for it and give me a chit. Word came down the pipe that he wasn't going to sign for it. So I said, "I'm sorry, but the

C.O. must sign for it. It isn't his to have." My M.O. advised me that I had better give it to him. I thought about it overnight; and then I had an idea. The next morning, I got on my bicycle, put the flying jacket in the carrier, rode to the stores and handed it over to the sergeant in charge. "Here's Sgt. so-and-so's jacket. If the C.O. wants it, he can draw it from stores." The sergeant replied, "I wondered how long it would be before you came." So I won that little battle. After all, right is right.

By this time, things had settled down with Sheila. She had had a brief friendship with an army guy stationed somewhere near Bebington, but he had been moved, and so that had fizzled out. I was able to visit her by taking the train from Halton in Buckinghamshire, getting off at Rickmansworth, and going the short distance to where Sheila was billeted. Then an edict came down—I think D-Day was coming up—that we were no longer allowed to travel by train—but that applied only to the main lines. So I decided to take a branch line that runs to Chesham. If I rode my bike to Chesham, I could put it in the guardsvan (caboose) and get off at Rickmansworth, where I would be almost there. Of course I would need a pass to leave the camp. When I approached the Warrant Officer, he asked me why I was going and reminded me that we were limited to 15 miles. I said, "That's okay." So he gave me the pass, but told me NOT to get caught. Fortunately this Warrant Officer had gone to Hulme Grammar school—the same school that I had attended in Manchester—and we had a bit of friendship going.

There were two sergeants on staff who were from London, but had never been anywhere else other than Halton. They had been going back to London on the train each weekend. So when this edict about not using the trains came out, they wanted to know how I was managing to see Sheila. I said that if they would each bring a bicycle, I would show them how. Of course they never did.

Sheila and friends at R.A.F. Headquarters, London 1944.

One difficulty that Sheila and I had to contend with was obtaining leave at the same time. You could put in for a leave, but you might not get it. Once when I was at York, we both put in for leaves and luckily both leaves were granted. We planned to go up to Millom in Cumberland, because I knew the vicar there. He had previously been in Fallowfield in Manchester and had told me to come up anytime—that he would provide accommodations. So I telephoned to say that I would be coming and bringing Sheila. He promised to put us up, but when the time came and I telephoned just to make sure, he said he could not accommodate us because he had given the space to a group of evacuees from Newcastle. So there we were—both with leave passes and nowhere to go.

I don't remember how I managed to get in touch with Sheila, but I did. We decided that she would get on the train in London and that I would travel from York to Preston, where we would hopefully meet. I arrived first. When her train arrived, I couldn't see her, but decided to get on anyway. When the train reached Lancaster, I looked for her up and down the platform. Finally I saw her hanging out of a window at the far end of the train.

We arrived at Millom in the wee hours of the morning with nowhere to stay. We found one hotel, but although the doors were wide open, there was no one about. Next we walked to another hotel up on Holborn Hill. Again, there was no one to be found. Then we spotted a man up on a ladder cleaning windows, and we asked if he knew anywhere we could stay. We were both in uniform, and he said, "Mrs. Robinson up on Holborn Hill has somebody from the R.A.F. staying with her. Maybe she has a room." So we trekked up to number 73, Holborn Hill and knocked on the door. Mrs. Robinson answered and said that she could put us up, as the people who had been with her had just left. Our bedrooms were up in the attic, on each side of the corridor, with an ornate Victorian water jug and basin in each. We discovered matching chamber pots under the beds, as the toilet was down three flights of stairs and out into the back yard.

We stayed there for about a week, climbing up Black Combe (1969 ft.), and visiting Eskdale and Ennerdale. Mrs. Robinson fed us very well. We also visited Sam Taylor, the vicar, who apologized for not being able to put us up. Sam was a pretty straightforward guy. We attended his church on Sunday, and his sermon was about promiscuity. There I was sitting with Sheila, and I felt like crawling under the pew. Sheila took it well, however, and we said nothing about it when we spoke to Sam Taylor afterwards. All in all, we had a wonderful stay at Mrs. Robinson's and would return many times in the future with our children. Following our week away, Sheila and I returned to our separate stations, she to Ruislip in London, and I to York.

Black Combe viewed from Silecroft, near Millom in Cumberland.

On another occasion when I was staying in Halton, Sheila applied for a leave and was refused. However, I had seen a notice in office records that were posted in various camps from time to time, that wives could get leave when their husbands were on leave. I was already on my way and it was too late to stop things; so I went to Ruislip and said to the Adjutant, "What's this? My wife can't get leave? Have you read 28 group orders? There they are on your desk."

"All right, but I'll have to get authorization from the Air Ministry."

Instead of phoning the Air Ministry, they sent a wireless signal. It was only about 25–30 miles to London, but they sent a SIGNAL! And we had to wait for the lousy signal to get back before we could get away. We got away about a day and a half later.

After all this trouble, we decided that we had better get married, so we fixed the date for October 16, 1943. Bud Cross, who had introduced us, agreed to be our best man. When the time drew near and I hadn't heard from Bud for quite a long time, I started to get worried. I tried to contact him by phone, but because it was war time, I really had no idea where he was. Eventually I was able to reach him.

"You what …? Can't get leave…? ASK OFF OR JUST COME!"

It was almost the day of my wedding, and I needed a best man. My Mum and Dad were coming down from Manchester; Sheila's sister Doreen was coming; everything was set up; but Bud might not be able to come. So I said to one of the Corporals at the camp, "Will you do me a very big favour?"

"What's that?"

"Be best man at my wedding on Saturday in London?"

He almost swallowed his tonsils, but he agreed to come.

"I'll be in London on Saturday, and I'll meet you at Baker Street Station."

I set off on Friday in my best uniform and stayed in the Y.M.C.A. When I went to bed, I put my pants under the blanket to press them, but they came out in the morning looking like a concertina. I had to get them pressed somehow. By 7:00 a.m. I had managed to find a laundry-type place nearby and advertising something about suits being pressed. The owner sent me down a winding, circular stair and asked me to throw my pants up to him, which I did. Then he pressed them for me, and that was another hurdle surmounted.

Next I went to Baker St. Station, looking for Mac, the airman who was to be my best man. Although the train was delayed, he did arrive, and we went to Lyons Corner House for a bite to eat before taking the train to Ruislip. The washroom in the place was like a telephone box—no room to smarten up. We did what we could, however, and then boarded the train. First it started, then stopped, then started again. It turned out that the line had been bombed the night before. We finally arrived at our destination at three o'clock—the very time the wedding was supposed to start.

It was a warm day, but wearing our great coats and carrying our gas masks with our steel helmets attached, we started to run up the hill to the church. The taxi man had picked Sheila up earlier—the fool—instead of making sure we were both there. So Sheila was hiding behind the door of the church. When we arrived, Mac was in such a state that they thought it was HE who was getting married. He had the ring, so I said, "Come on, Mac. We're on!" We threw our gas masks and steel helmets into the corner and marched straight up the aisle. Afterwards we enjoyed a nice little wedding meal, then travelled to Millom for our honeymoon on a leave that had been pre-arranged.

Peter and Sheila Beatson on their wedding day, Oct.16, 1943.

Bride and groom with wedding guests.

Chapter VI

In Chapter V, I mentioned being sent to the Chiltern Hills for a six-month course on tropical diseases, tropical medicine and general lab work. This course turned out to be comprehensive and interesting, though the officer in charge was not my friend Wing Commander Hackett, but an Air Commodore who hailed from Malta. This gentleman wasn't very nice; and our group tried to have as little as possible to do with him.

When we reported for work in the morning, he made us line up (as if on parade), salute and wait for dismissal before heading off to our labs. One day at lunch, having gone through this morning routine, I was crossing from our building to the Canteen with two others when who should come marching towards us but Mr. Maltese Air Commodore. There's a rule in the military that you salute whenever you pass an officer. However, there is also a rule that you salute only when wearing a hat, and none of us were wearing hats. As we passed the officer, therefore, I merely said, "Good morning, Sir," and we continued on our way.

When I returned from lunch, the Warrant Officer said, "What the hell have you been doing to the Old Man?"

"Haven't done anything to the Old Man."

"Not saluting him or something like that?"

I explained that I had already saluted him in the morning and that I hadn't ignored him, but had paid my respects.

"But everybody has to salute!"

The next day an order came down that everybody was to salute the officers at all times. Well, Halton was a pretty big camp, and this order lasted only a day and a half. Can you imagine? Every time an officer walked into a hangar, you were supposed to stop what you were doing and salute him—even if you were up on the wing of an airplane with tools in your hands. Ridiculous! I usually got on with my officers quite well—never tried to be awkward with them in front of others, but always treated them with respect. For that matter, they usually did the same with me. It is understood that if there's a Sergeant in charge of 10 men, a Flight Sergeant doesn't come in and bawl him out in front of them. If necessary, he takes the Sergeant aside and has his say privately because the Sergeant must retain his men's respect in order to do his job. I was always very careful about that sort of thing.

During my time at the Institute, I had to do a lot of studying, and I couldn't study where we were quartered—little houses that in peacetime had served as married quarters. Each building had three guys upstairs and another three down. So on nice spring or summer days, I would ride my bicycle into the nearby hills where I could stop by the roadside and do a bit of studying. Afterwards I would go to a local pub and enjoy a couple of jugs before returning to the camp.

On one occasion I found the pub absolutely packed with American servicemen, and I was the only one from the R.A.F. So no one would let me pay for a drink; they just kept buying them for me. In those days you couldn't really ask people what they were doing, but I did learn that they were all musicians, and I wondered if they might have been from Glen Miller's band, at the time touring England. Eventually, they put me on my bicycle, pointed me in the right direction, checked that I was balancing okay, and sent me on my way.

My room mates in those days can only be described as "plain miserable." One of them was a commercial traveller who hated being in the Armed Forces. The other was a "morbid histologist,' who worked on staff at the Institute and who, in civilian life, had done the same work. He was a dark, heavy-featured, lantern-jawed sort of man whom I had never seen smile—that is until one day when I encountered him coming down the corridor wringing his hands and wearing the broadest of smiles. "What's up?" I inquired.

"I've got a P.M. (post mortem)," he answered. Anyway, these were my room mates.

You will recall that I had had quite a few drinks with the Americans up in the hills. When I arrived back at the house, these two were in their beds either snoring or grumbling. So I devised a clever plan to get the beggars out. I picked up two pint mugs which we kept in our room, filled one with water and left the other empty. Then I stood beside one bed and began to pour the water slowly from one mug to the other, all the while saying things like, "Come on, Bert. You must want to go to the toilet; you must have to pee." Back and forth—back and forth with the water! Eventually, he got up, sort of smiled, and then laughed out loud. Then the other guy called out from his bed, "It won't work with me." So I stood beside his bed and did the same thing: back and forth—back and forth. Just when I had almost given up, he shouted, "Dammit!" Then he too got up and went downstairs to the toilet. I guess my practical joke had broken the ice. When I returned to the same pub the next day, the Americans were still there, but when returned to my quarters and tried to get into bed, I couldn't. The bed had been apple-pied—made up in such a way that I couldn't get my feet down. To make matters worse, as I struggled to climb in, the bed collapsed onto the floor. It seems they'd done a good one back on me. But that was all right—just a bit of fun.

Meanwhile my course was going well, and I was finding it very interesting. However, when it came time for my examination, guess who was going to be my examiner—none other than Mr. Maltese officer. Knowing he would be the one, I made a special point of learning extras—much more than was required. Sure enough, he asked me extra questions as I sat in front of him for the oral examination: What would I do about this? What temperature would be appropriate for that? Blah, blah, blah! At one point he even stomped off to the lab to check on one of my answers. In the end, he gave me a mark of 78 per cent—earned, I might say, under duress. Not bad, considering!

My next posting was to Cleveleys hospital, formerly a hotel on the sea front called the Cleveleys' Hyatt. I stayed there for only a week, filling in for a Lab Tech who was sick, but I had to keep my wits about me as we were very, very busy. During my stay, I was billeted with a retired postman and his wife, who made me very welcome. One night, they invited me to go bowling, where I won a pair of Apostle spoons, which I still have today.

After Cleveleys, I received a more permanent posting to Rauceby Hospital in Sleaford, Lincolnshire. It had formerly been a mental hospital, built in the early 1900s. Nearby was Cranwell, a permanent R.A.F station many years before the War. Although Cranwell, a fairly large station, had its own sick bay, Rauceby served as its main hospital. The hospital itself was quite large, with modern extensions on the end and side. It also had up-to-date equipment. In addition to Cranwell military station, Rauceby served Yorkshire and Lincolnshire for general ailments, as well as for aircraft accidents. Situated on the east coast of England where the night bombers would return from the Continent—some making it, others not— we were always busy. Sometimes our team would be up all night. Among other things, we were a burns centre, as a lot of crews returning from bombing flights sustained bad burns when their planes caught fire—either on the way down or after crashing. Some men were badly disfigured or lost limbs. For burns, we worked in conjunction with East Grinstead down in Kent, the number-one burns centre in the country. Dr. McKindoe, who visited us once, was their top burns specialist. Some of the badly burned airmen had once been good-looking guys, as evidenced by the photographs at their bedsides. However, once their girlfriends or wives had visited them and seen their disfigurement, some no longer wanted to be with them. These women couldn't bear to look at their men, never mind stay with them on a permanent basis. Naturally, this was very demoralizing to the airmen.

Rauceby Hospital staff 1944.

Pathology Lab staff, Rauceby Hospital.
Peter is first right in the front row.

I remember a crash involving three or four airmen and one airman in particular. He was terribly congested—unable to get the phlegm out of his throat. We had almost given up on him until one of our staff, a clinical photographer, got an idea. He took an enema syringe, put one end in the patient's mouth, and pumped and pumped until all the mucous had come out. By the next morning the patient was looking a lot better.

Another memory involves a WAAF who had sustained a spinal injury in a truck accident. She used to go into the wards in her wheelchair to visit some of the badly burned airmen. It really boosted their morale to be visited by this girl, who was quite good looking and wasn't frightened by their appearance. The eventual cure for her spinal injury was rather unique. Rauceby had very large bathtubs, which they would fill with isotonic saline (nine per cent saline) for soaking the clothes off injured airmen before treating their burns. For some reason, she received the same treatment, and it apparently helped, for she learned to walk again.

I also recall an occasion when our Pathologist, a Dr. O'Connor from Australia, asked me for assistance. When I inquired as to the nature of the case, he said it was a full post mortem on one of our nursing sisters, who (it was thought) had committed suicide by drug overdose. I winced when I heard this. Luckily I did not know her very well, but that was a tough one for me.

On the lighter side, I recall an incident involving another sister, one who had all the appearance of a "woman of the old school." She had a thin, unpleasant countenance, and used to be very heavy handed and officious with the airmen, some of whom had served in the desert against Rommel. In response to her ways, the men would throw thermometers across the ward and engage in other wild behaviours during her shift. It so happened one day that she got a posting overseas and required a medical, including a urinalysis, When her sample came to me in the pathology lab, I was surprised to see spermatozoa when I looked at it under the microscope. So I consulted the pathologist, who instructed me to put it down as "normal flora." You never know, do you!

On another occasion, our entire team of lab technologists—including a Squadron Leader, a Corporal, and several others—was at work in the lab wearing our white coats, so that you couldn't tell anybody's rank. The Corporal was an airman who played guitar—a six-foot, good-looking guy from Newcastle in Northumberland, very broadly spoken, with a heavy northern accent. Suddenly an army Lieutenant burst into the lab.

"Could anybody tell me the way to Rauceby Hall? I say, who's in charge here?"

The Corporal drew himself up to his full height and said in perfectly cultured English, "Oh, you…you came from Grantham, I suppose; you didn't see the sign to Ancaster when you were on the way, did you? I suppose you did see that, did you? And you <u>did</u> see the other sign too. I suppose you saw that, did you?"

As he went on like this for two or three minutes, the army Lieutenant shrank smaller and smaller. Finally he burst back out of out of the lab. Meanwhile, "Old Digger," our Squadron Leader, had not said a word.

In 1945, my wife, Sheila, left the Armed Forces because she was expecting a baby (our daughter, Jackie). Prior to the birth, Sheila came to Sleaford, where we stayed with a Mrs. Hickersly and her husband and I rode back and forth to Rauceby Hospital on an old motor bike. On one occasion, Sheila and I headed out on the bike for Grantham. We were almost there when the clutch cable broke. Sheila got off and she sat on a wall beside the road while I tended to the bike. I managed to jump start it; then ran with it and jumped back on. When I reached Grantham, nobody wanted to look at it, as it was Saturday. Finally, I found a blacksmith who was willing to help. Meanwhile, Sheila was waiting on the wall, halfway between Sleaford and Grantham. At one point, a lady came out of her house to ask Sheila if she was all right. Eventually, however, I returned and we rode home safely.

Another place we used to go was Boston—the real Boston—about 30 miles from Sleaford. In fact, if you stood on the roof of the hospital, you could see the tower of "Boston Stump." Boston's cathedral was given this name because its tower was never properly finished. We used to go there from time to time for a nice meal. Sheila and I had found a little restaurant where two old ladies would cook pigeon for us. It made a really nice outing, and if we wanted extra eggs, we would walk to a little farm nearby where we could get them. After Jackie was born, we would push her all the way in the pram to get the eggs, which were rationed at the time. We would pay something for the eggs, and they'd give us a sit-down tea, making sure we were fortified for the walk home. I'm sure they made no money on us, but they were lovely people.

In March of 1945, the War ended in Europe, and there were big VE Day celebrations everywhere. We staged our own celebration at Rauceby. There was a band, made up of hospital staff; various sporting events; and a big dinner in the dining hall. Normally our hospital food was abominable, but this time the cooks went all out, and I'd never seen such a spread—though it was still ration time. My brother, David, joined us for the celebration, as did my mother. In fact, David entered one of the races. They wanted him to start at the front of the pack because he was so young. However, David refused and started at the back. By the end, he had absolutely walked away with the race. Then he ran another one, also starting at the back, with the same result. David was a member of the R.A.F. where he was a Physical Training Instructor (P.T.I.); so he was in excellent shape. I recall that when it came time to eat, David hid extra food under his chair so he wouldn't lose it.

When it came time to go home to Sleaford, we realized we had a problem: there were four of us to go back and only one motor bike. However, the distance was only two or three miles. So I took Sheila first, then my mother; then I ran out of gas. What to do? I went back to the lab and retrieved pint bottles of both alcohol and benzene. Then I put both into the tank and shook the whole bike. It worked! Boy, did that bike go! My mother and I shot back to Sleaford as if we were riding a rocket.

Before Jackie was born, Sheila travelled to Manchester to stay with my mother. Following the birth, Sheila and the baby returned to Sleaford. Jackie was christened in an 11th century church, where her name can be found in the registry book. We rented a little house, right beside the River Slea—really only a brook, but very nice, with trout, swans and a little bridge leading to the main street with its Woolworth's and other shops. There was also a moving-picture house. At the time, coal was on the ration and I wasn't able to get any, even though I had gone to the coalman and explained about the baby. Then Sheila and I thought of raking around in the coal shed at the bottom of our yard. By doing this, we found enough coal to warm the place until we could get coupons. After that, we managed okay. Before our arrival, the house had been rented by an airman, a Sergeant, and his family. When I saw him at camp, he looked very smart—with polished buttons and the like. However, the condition of his house was terrible, and we had a big cleaning job to do. Later, when our landlord came to collect the rent, his eyes nearly popped out when he saw how nice everything looked. Of course, our furniture was old, and we didn't have much, but the place now looked clean and cared for.

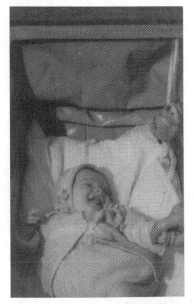

Jacqueline Ann Beatson, b. Dec. 5, 1945.

Next came VJ day, the end of the war with Japan. So we had another celebration—also with lots of food—in the dining hall. The officers even removed their ties and rode around the dance floor on their motor bikes. It was near pandemonium, but a great party nonetheless.

After VJ Day, there was a big dance at Rauceby Hospital when unfortunately the whole hall went ablaze. The fire may have been caused by something like electrical wiring, but the band members were blamed for smoking on stage. There was pine panelling all the way up to the ceiling, and the wood must have been very dry, having been built circa 1910. Needless to say, the hall went up like a tinderbox. The big dome at the top fell in, and fire trucks came from miles around to fight the blaze. I remember standing on the roof of a corridor, holding a hose with one of the firemen, when I noticed some black objects floating down. When I realized what they were—slates falling off the roof—I got out of there very quickly. Fortunately they managed to keep the fire from going to the corridors where the patients were. Also, the band instruments were stored away from the fire; so none of them were lost. Nevertheless, all the band members, with the exception of the guitar player were sent to far away places.

The guitar player had been on leave at the time of the fire, and when he came back, he found himself without a band. This man happened to sleep in the bunk next to mine, and he asked me if I knew how to play anything. I replied that I had "tootled about" on the clarinet, but that I didn't have my own instrument anymore. He then asked if I might be able to play the drums. I said that I'd be willing to give it a try. He also recruited a saxophone player, and two others, and I began going up into the band room to practise on the drums using a metronome. However, I found I wasn't getting anywhere; so I went to the Navy, Army & Air Force Institutes (N.A.A.F.I.) Club in Sleaford and sat in the wings offstage watching the drummer. His name was Ozzie Nobel, a professional drummer who, in civilian life, had done solo acts up and down the country. One day, as I was watching him, he suddenly walked off stage, handed me the sticks, and said, "Now, you have a go." I had no time to get stage fright: the dance floor was packed, and I guess he knew what he was doing, because the band was playing a slow number.

Shortly afterwards four or five of us formed a new band, which included an Irish pianist with a very short temper. At first, being new to the drums, I didn't keep time properly. Instead of listening to the rhythm of the pianist's left hand, I was following the melody of his right hand, which is no good with dance music; and the Irish pianist was starting to get angry. I was determined, however, to be the boss; I thought to myself, "This time you'll play it my way. I'll play it the way I want it; I'll set the time." Well, I did, and he said, "That's fine, that's great." It suddenly clicked that I could keep the tempo.

Navy, Army and Air Force Institutes. *1944 – 1945*

N.A.A.F.I. CLUB, SLEAFORD
Forthcoming Entertainments

SATURDAY, MARCH 23rd	**WEDNESDAY, MARCH 27th**
3.30 to 5.30 The Dansant. Stanley Robinson and his Band	3.30 to 5.30 R.A.F College Light Orchestra, Under direction of L.A.C. Thomas Geradine, F.T.C.L.
5.30 to 6.30 Dancing Lessons by Cpl. Boyd	6.45 to 9.45 Variety. "The Masqueraders"
6.45 to 9.45 Dance. Stanley Robinson and his Band	**THURSDAY, MARCH 28th GUEST NIGHT.**
	3.30 to 5.30 Radio Request Programme
SUNDAY, MARCH 24th	7 p.m. Gramophone Recital for Members of Music Circle in Music Room
3.30 to 5.30 The Selmer Trio The Dansant and Medley of Music	6.45 to 9.45 Dance. Stanley Robinson and his Band Featuring: "Dusty Miller"
6.45 to 9.45 Dance. Selmer Four	**FRIDAY, MARCH 29th**
	3.30 to 5.30 Radio Request Programme
MONDAY, MARCH 25th	5.30 to 6.30 Dancing Classes by Cpl. Boyd
6.45 to 9.45 Dance. Billy Cowell and his Band	6.45 to 9.45 Dance. "The Pathogens" Under direction of Sgt. Peter Beatson
TUESDAY, MARCH 26th	**SATURDAY, MARCH 30th**
Whist Drive in Music Room	3.30 to 5.30 The Dansant. Stanley Robinson and his Band
Darts Match in Games Room	5.30 to 6.30 Dancing Lessons by Cpl. Boyd
Table Tennis Match in Ballroom	6.45 to 9.45 Dance. Stanley Robinson and his Band

"Forthcoming entertainments," N.A.A.F.I. Club, Sleaford.

N.A.A.F.I. Club, Sleaford.

We played quite a few times at the Navy, Army & Air Force Club, a beautiful place in Sleaford that had once been a Corn Exchange. They had converted it to a club with a dance floor big enough to hold 200 people and a large stage. Money had been no object at the time: the job just had to be done for the Armed Forces. Our little band also played in village halls, as well as other Air Force stations in the surrounding area. We always had our program written out beforehand, and since two of us worked in the pathology lab at the hospital, we called ourselves the Pathogens—a unique name that went down quite well. We became quite popular. I played with the Pathogens and lived in the same house in Sleaford until I was demobilized, at which point I had to report to another base and hand in my uniform. I also received a few weeks' pay along with an ill-fitting suit and a Trillby hat, but never a thank you. I was paid exactly £81—I have it on paper—after six-and-a-half years! I didn't find this particularly generous.

The Pathogens, Rauceby Hospital 1945.

Release document for Sgt. E. P. Beatson.

I did keep the drum set, however, taking it to my mother's on Whitby Road in Manchester, where I, Sheila and the baby went to live for a time. I also placed an ad in the *Manchester Evening News:* "Drummer available, with transport." It was just after the War, and anyone in a band who could provide the transportation was at a premium. One day a guy came knocking at my door and asked, "Can you play with us on Saturday at Co-op Hall in Platt Fields?" I replied that I could and asked for the details. When I arrived and mounted the stage to start playing, the accordion player asked me where I worked. I replied, "At Imperial Chemical Industries (I.C.I.)." He said, "So do I." Next the pianist and the bass player turned around, each of them saying in turn, "So do I." It turned out that we all worked for the same company, only they were at Blakely and I was at Trafford Park. So we formed a band and invited several others join us, including sax and trumpet players.

We played in and around Manchester for quite a few years. Each year, for example, we played the Grand Hotel for their Christmas dance. Even after my family moved to Macclesfield, 23 miles to Manchester, I continued to play. Some of our gigs were bow-tie-and-tails events, and I found these very enjoyable. Others were less so. On one occasion, we were alternating with an Irish band for a St. Patrick's dance. While we played, they would go down to the pub; and vice versa. This went on until midnight, at which point someone asked, "Aren't you coming for a drink?"

"It's midnight! Ah, OK."

We went around the corner to a place called the Swan and knocked three times (though we didn't ask for Joe). The landlord put his head outside, looked up and down the street, and then said, "Get inside!" He led us to a back room where there was a whole crowd of people drinking it up. There were two girls in the group, who in the course of our conversation said something about uniforms. I supposed they were nurses. When I later offered them a ride home, they accepted, but added a caveat, "But don't forget, no funny business—we're policewomen. And we've already got your car number."

Another time we played at a wedding in a church hall in north Manchester. Our pianist, Norman Shaw, and our sax player, Bert Howarth, were with me, as well as a trumpet player. When Norman touched the piano keys, the sound that came out was horrible. However, we played the best we could. To make matters worse, there was some sort of fracas going on between the two families, and we had quite a job getting them to join in. So we played things like round dances, where everyone moved around the floor until they eventually paired off. Shortly after our half-time break a fight broke out, and I could see that the situation wasn't going to improve. Since we always asked for our money at half time and we had already been paid, I told the lads to pack up their things quietly and get ready to leave.

"What do you mean, we're leaving?"

"Get ready to move."

I had the worst job because of all the pieces in my drum set. However, I managed to whittle it down and pack some of the things away. Then I quietly brought my old Sunbeam car around to the door and parked it. When we finished the next number, I said, "Right, lads! Now!" We dashed down the stairs to the street, rolling the big drum ahead of us—blum, blum, blum. Then we put everything in the car and started off. Meanwhile some of the wedding guests had also rushed down the stairs, and were banging their fists on the Sunbeam as we drove away. Too bad! There was no way I would carry on there and possibly have our instruments smashed. It wasn't worth the trouble.

We had other adventures and experienced many ups and downs from 1946–1965. In 1965 I flew to Canada—ending almost 20 years of playing, not counting the years I was with the Pathogens in the R.A.F.

Chapter VII

Following demobilization, Sheila and I returned with the baby to Sleaford because we were still renting the house there. I didn't have to look for a job, because following the War in Britain, you were guaranteed a position with the company that had employed you before you enlisted. I had worked for Boots the Chemist, a large retail pharmaceutical company. They offered me my former position at the pharmacy in Sale. However this job no longer appealed to me—serving behind the counter or "counter jumping," as I used to call it. I'd learned a lot since then and had done a great deal of lab work during my military service; so I asked Boots if I could work in one of their labs, and they agreed. They subsequently assigned me to a research lab at their headquarters in Nottingham. So Sheila and I went looking for houses in that community. At the time, new houses were being built, and a semi-detached house could be purchased for about £900. I had been paid £10 per week in the Armed Forces, but when I went to Nottingham to see what they were prepared to pay, they offered me only £5. Unfortunately, I had to take it because I had no other job offers, and this made buying a house out of our reach. So Sheila and Jackie went to live with my mother in Manchester, while I had to find separate accommodations in Nottingham where I worked.

Our son, Rodger, was born in 1946. At the time, I was paying my landlady £2.5 per week, which left only £2.5 for Sheila and the two children. As a result, we were forced to draw upon our small savings. When I asked for a raise, I was refused. To make matters worse, my landlady, a Mrs. Best (who modelled herself after Queen Victoria—black dresses and all), was slowly starving me. She provided a mean breakfast, no lunch, and a thin slice of ham with a slice of tomato for supper. Once she went away for a week on business, leaving her daughter and granddaughter in charge. What a change! I had bacon-and-eggs tea brought up to my room—a totally different scene.

For transportation, I managed to obtain a motor bike with very few miles on it that had been used for dispatch during the War. I would travel on it from Nottingham to Manchester each weekend, an interesting and scenic ride over the hills. I would leave each Friday night after work and return very early Monday morning—a distance of about 70 miles each way. I had to make sure I set off in good time, in order to make allowances for the mechanics of my bike, as well as the weather.

On one occasion, after I had used the gear box to slow me down on the steep descent into Ashbourne, the engine started misfiring and banging as I drove into town. It took me a long time to get it going again, and when I finally did, the engine was still making all sorts of noise. In spite of this, I managed to arrive at work in Nottingham by 8:30 a.m. Another time, as I was returning to work from the Macclesfield direction, I encountered a motor coach lying on its side and leaning into the ditch, and I could see the passengers sitting in a nearby field, some of them injured. I looked at this mess and thought, "There are too many here for me to do anything on my own." So I sped down into Ashbourne, knocked at a policeman's house, pounded repeatedly until he answered the door, then telephoned for an ambulance. Fortunately, I learned that an ambulance was already on its way.

At one point my employers at the lab asked me to punch a time clock, and I refused. I said if they couldn't trust me to do my work, then I was not their man. Of course, I had to make sure I was never late. I also understood that soon I would have to look for another job. Fortunately, my brother knew someone in Manchester who worked at Imperial Chemical Industries. When they offered me a job at Trafford Park, I accepted. Not only was the salary higher than Boots was paying me by £6 per week, but I would be able to live at my mother's with Sheila and the children. Boots subsequently offered to increase my pay, but it still wasn't enough. I started my new job at Trafford Park in 1946.

I.C.I. laboratory where Peter worked.

One day, as I rode to work on my motor bike, I attempted to pass a coal lorry with a flat bed. As I began to pass, he suddenly turned into a side road without signaling. I might have been able to get around him anyway, but I could see ahead of me a post box at the corner; so I was forced to choose between hitting the truck and hitting the post box. I caught the truck somewhere near its rear wheel, and flew off my bike. As I rose into the air, I could see the bike following behind me, and I remember thinking, "I hope that so-and-so doesn't catch me up." I landed on the road like a cat—on all fours. Then I confronted the driver, who apologetically offered to take me to work. I said not a word to Sheila about this incident.

As a result of this accident, the foot rests on my bike were badly bent, but I managed to straighten them up and make my bike mobile again. Some time later I sold the bike, though I don't remember exactly why or when. Certainly, Jackie and Rodger were beginning to grow up, and there was no way we could all travel together on one motor bike. Whatever the reason, I bought a little SS1 car, the first of the Jaguars. It was a neat little car with a four-cylinder standard engine, and would hold four people. Of course it had a stick shift, and there was a luggage compartment on the back. Later in this chapter, I will tell you more about the various vehicles that I owned during these early years.

With respect to my work at the lab, the discovery of penicillin (quite by accident) in 1945 by Alexander Fleming had generated a great deal of interest in fungi. In both the United States and Britain, there was a rush to examine many other kinds of fungi to see if they had the same activity. Dr. Fleming had even visited Trafford Park to see the work that we were doing, and I had met him on that occasion. To identify fungi, you had to look at them under a microscope. I had been asked to look after photography and some other aspects of this work; so I built a dark room, purchased the necessary supplies, and obtained a Leica camera and adaptor. I would look down the microscope, focus the image on the ground-glass screen of the adaptor, then replace it with the Leica camera. In this manner, I was able to produce photographs of the various fungi in quick succession, using 35mm film. In fact, in 1947, I published an internal article on the procedure, complete with illustrations.

Leica photo of penicillin taken by Peter Beatson.

At the time, there were very few reference books on fungi. We did have one book by an Italian researcher named Sicardo, who had done a lot of work identifying fungi before the War. His book contained colour plates showing the various fungi. It became our responsibility to identify a whole lot of fungi that people had brought in from the fields. We would grow some of them on culture dishes, and others in stirred flasks. Then we would take the liquor from those flasks and check it against various bacteria, including tuberculosis. Some of this work was done at Blakely, another section of I.C.I. across town. However, a number of the staff there wouldn't touch it because we were using viable TB. So I used to go over to Blakely twice a week, get all gowned up, and do the assays using human TB. Why was I willing while others were not? Perhaps it was because of my experiences in bacteriology during the War. In the end, we didn't come up with anything significant other than streptomycin and griseofulvin—only two of the thousands of fungi that were tested in the US and Britain for over three years by teams of people trying to find a wonder cure. Eventually they gave up on fungi and began to fold our section.

After the section was closed, I was transferred to Blakely in the pharmaceutical research department where the task at hand was to develop new products for the market. The products had to be made, mixed, tested and then go to clinical trials. I was successful in developing dispersible penicillin for intermammary use in cows. Farmers of the day had been injecting penicillin into cows' udders in an oily suspension. Following the injections, they were unable to use the milk for a week or so, because the penicillin would still be there. The formula I invented was dispersible—the penicillin would be dispersed within 72 hours, and I held the patent for its use in the U.K. I did the same sort of work at Blakely for quite awhile.

Meanwhile, Sheila and I, along with our two children, continued to live with my mother in Manchester. In February 1950, I heard rumours that the research lab where I worked would be moving out to Wilmslow, about 20 miles to the south of Manchester. Since we still didn't have our own home, we thought we should look for one in that area. However, we discovered that the prices at Wilmslow were out of this world and certainly out of our reach. Instead, we began to look around Macclesfield to see if we could find anything there. We were eventually successful in finding a house close to Macclesfield in a village called Rainow. The name of the house was "Springmount." The owner, a retired school teacher named Mrs. Wallace, had allowed it to deteriorate into terrible shape. However, it was available at a price we could afford and was situated in a very scenic part of the country. We purchased the house in 1950 for £900. Subsequently, when we met the seller at her door, she was wearing a black cashmere top, with a sack tied around her middle, and some sort of skirt. Her hair was grey and wispy and her eyes were strange. She needed only a broomstick and she could have taken off.

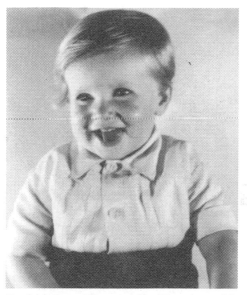

Rodger Peter Beatson, b. Nov. 5, 1946.

Rodger Peter Beatson.

Macclesfield, Cheshire.

"Springmount," the Beatson home in Rainow.

One of the men I worked with at the lab was a chemist named Jerry Harris. He had a Ph.D. from Oxford and was a really good scout. He would come to work on a little BSA Bantam motorcycle, wearing a bowler hat, with his briefcase tied on the back. He was a really gentle man, an easy-going sort, but his boss at the lab, a chemist in charge of the section, was giving him a hard time—in front of other staff. I told Jerry he shouldn't allow this—that if his boss had anything to say to him, he should say it in private. However, Jerry never did anything about it, other than trying to get his section separated from this boss, whose name was Calam. However, I.C.I. wouldn't go for it, and Jerry eventually left for another job in Terre Haute, Indiana, U.S.A. Prior to that, however, he used to come and help us decorate our new home, "Springmount." He stippled the walls for us, and did all sorts of other jobs—he was a really good person. Over the years we lived there, we continued to make small improvements so that "Springmount" gradually got better and better.

**Sheila (left) with sister Doreen (centre)
and friend on lane near "Springmount."**

Family admiring the view behind "Springmount."

Peter's mother with Jackie and Rodger at "Springmount."

Rainow Village, Cheshire.

Jerry Harris, Peter's boss at I.C.I.

During the same period, I began to purchase various old motor cars and fix them up. I have already mentioned the Jaguar, my very first motor car. I bought it from a man who lived in Fallowfield, near my Mum. I had only had it for a day or two when I drove into Stockport and it quit in the middle of the main square. I discovered that the crown pin on the back axle had broken. So I telephoned the man I had bought it from, and he fixed it at no charge. Following this incident, however, the car continued to quit on me for no apparent reason. I couldn't figure it out. On one occasion, we had driven it into Bebington and had decided to use the Mersey Tunnel. We were right at the bottom of the tunnel when the car decided to quit. The traffic could scarcely get by. So we had to be towed and pay a fine. Although we subsequently replaced the leads and plugs, the car quit on us again as we headed for Bebington on another outing. I remember it had rained and we had just driven through a puddle when the engine stopped. When I lifted the hood and examined the engine, I realized that the design was faulty. The distributor came out of the side of the engine block right behind the front wheel. Of course, when the front wheels hit a puddle of water, the water would splash up onto the distributor, and that would be it. So I removed the distributor cap, wiped it with my handkerchief, and thus solved the immediate problem. We were on our way again. Following this incident, I put a little shield around the distributor to protect it from any water that splashed up.

I used the knowledge gained by this experience a couple of times in the future. On one occasion, I was in Wales with my brother-in-law, Laurie. We had just dashed through a patch of road where a stream had overflowed its banks, when his car quit. I went out into the pouring rain and cleaned the distributor, after which we were able to continue on our journey. On another occasion, I helped a motorist in New York State in similar circumstances. I had observed his car come through a quantity of water and then quit. So I explained to him what had likely happened and showed him what to do.

I should have kept this car longer, but I was frightened that the axle was about to go again. At the time, I didn't know enough about the structure of cars to make a proper judgment: that there has to be some give in the coupling between the prop shaft and the rear pinion and that there are different designs for this area. In reality my car would have been okay, and I needn't have worried. However, I made the mistake of selling it and exchanging it for another car. The worst part of this deal was that I bought my next car after sunset. I have since learned that you should never buy a car in the dark.

The car I bought was a Standard, and it looked alright. The engine sounded good, but after I had brought it home, it turned out to be a disaster. First of all, although it was a Standard nine, box-shaped car, the body sank so much that it was resting on the rear springs. Secondly, the cylinder head on the engine was patched up with a plumber's solder—it was really bad. Once, after cleaning it up, I and my friend Roger Unsworth (who lived just around the corner) took it to Chester for a run. To our dismay, it used a quart of oil to get there and another quart to get home, and Chester was only 30 miles away. After this, I knew I had to sell it, but I couldn't sell it to an individual. So I took it to a garage in Chorlton. The dealer there sold me a Morris 10/4, built in 1934. This car had a better body, but the engine big ends were square; so it knocked and refused to pull uphill. We did get it fixed, however, and drove it for awhile. I once took Sheila and the children in this car to Millom in Cumberland.

1934 Morris 10/4.

After I sold the Morris, I bought a motor bike with a side car, a BSA Sloper. The engine, 500 cc, was sloping in the frame. It had a hand change on the tank, but no foot change. We drove it up to Millom with panniers on the back and stuffed into the nose of the side car. The two kids sat in the middle of the side car, and Sheila on the pillion. We had lots of good fun, except the day we travelled over Hard Knot Pass, which is quite steep. The road was surfaced on one side, but shale on the other. We were travelling on the incline and doing quite well until the engine revs began to build up and the clutch to slip. We returned to the bottom of the hill and tried again and again, but the bike couldn't make the climb. So Sheila and the kids got out and waited by the side of the road while I started from the bottom by myself. When I reached the point where they were waiting, I had instructed them to push. I don't remember who pushed, but the bike did make it to the top of the hill, and then we all clambered back in for the descent. Unfortunately, the road on the other side was nothing but loose shale. I had to drive down the slope in first gear with the lifter up and the brakes on. Fortunately, we made it down, but the next day as I was going to Conisten, I heard a "clump, clump." A cog had broken and come off in the gear box, and there was nothing in Millom to fix it.

BSA Sloper motor bike with side car.

The only place I was sure I could find the part I needed was Manchester. So I left the family in Millom, and took the bus to Manchester, a tedious journey. Once there, I went down to City Road, where I knew there would be all sorts of parts. There I purchased a new cog for my BSA 1929 Sloper. My Manchester friend, Roger Unsworth, drove me on his motor bike back to Millom with the spare part. The Sloper subsequently gave me good service, with only a few little incidents here and there.

My next purchase was another motor bike, a 600cc single cylinder Panther. The cylinder was inclined and formed part of the frame. It was a really good work horse, and I rode it daily from Manchester to Trafford Park and back. After our move, I rode it from "Springmount" in Rainow to Trafford Park. Like the BSA Sloper, it was a motor bike with side car, and we also used it as a family vehicle. We even used it once to tour Wales. However on the way back from Wales, it rained and rained, and we were forced to sit in a pool of water. So I decided to look for something else that would keep us dry.

Panther motor bike.

Panther motor bike with side car.

I found it in a Morgan three-wheeler. It had a soft top, a hood, two seats in front and two small seats behind. It also had a chain drive to a single rear wheel at the back. As with my previous purchases, it was in poor shape; so I stripped it down, taking the entire body off the frame and putting it back together. I also painted it, and eventually it looked quite good.

Morgan three-wheeler before restoration.

Morgan after restoration by Peter.

One problem with three-wheelers, however, is that they make it hard to miss obstructions on the road. If there is a pothole, one wheel or the other is bound to hit it. In this way, it was troublesome. Another problem was the engine, a V-twin matchless engine at the front. Once I laid it out on the kitchen table at "Springmount," and I could see gouge marks on the table. It also caused me similar problems to the one I'd had with the SS car, but in this case, the oil was getting into the distributor through the bushing. It was a horizontal bushing in which the oil was gradually feeding through into the distributor cap, eventually making the car stop. I solved this problem by carrying with me a little spray bottle of carbon tetrachloride. If the oil went into the wrong place and caused the engine to quit, I would simply spray this into the distributor cap, and the Morgan would be fine for awhile until the same thing happened again. Eventually I sold the Morgan and bought the Panther motor bike and side car back again. Afterwards I drove it for quite awhile.

Eventually, however, I decided that I should have four wheels again. The family needed protection from the weather, and as I was still playing in the band, I needed a vehicle to carry my drum kit around. Once I had had to put the whole drum kit into the side car with all the rest of the band's paraphernalia, and arrive at a dance gig all suited up for motorcycling. Underneath, of course, was my dress suit and dickie bow. Usually, I left the drum kit at Jim's, a band member who lived in Manchester, and I would take the train from Macclesfield to Manchester and return at midnight. When I arrived back in Macclesfield, it would be about 12:40 a.m., and I would walk from Hibel Road Station up to Rainow, an uphill distance of about two and one-half miles. On some nights the walk was nice, but on others it was foggy. At any rate, this routine wasn't a long-term solution. I had to have four wheels.

My next vehicle was a square-bodied, black 1934 Hillman. The engine was good, but the brakes were useless. I think they were cable, with pre-stretched cables. I had to put little adjustors in to take up the slack, and as we drove along, we could hear a tinkle, tinkle sound. I used this car for band jobs and also for family holidays. All in all, it wasn't too bad. However, I do remember one incident involving Sheila's Mum, who was visiting us for a few days from Highcroft in the Wirral. We were driving around back of the hills by Goyt Valley and Pym's Chair when we encountered an especially steep hill. Suddenly the clutch wouldn't grip, and the brakes were no good. Meanwhile, the engine revs were building up, but the car wasn't moving forward. In fact, the car was starting to roll backwards. Eventually, it ran into a grassy bank, where it stopped. We tried and tried to get it away, using stones and pushing. Eventually we did get the car to the top of Pym's chair. Now what were we to do? Sheila's Mum was still sitting on the grass verge halfway down the hill. She wouldn't have been able to walk up to the top; so we linked arms in a fireman's chair and carried her. Afterwards, by judicious use of the gear box, we managed to get home via Whaley Bridge. Sheila's Mum never batted an eyelid or said anything. She must have enjoyed the outing.

I subsequently had to remove the clutch and was able to fix it in a neighbour's farmyard. The neighbour in question was a Mr. Starling, who owned a farm just down the road. It turned out that he was an engineer who worked at Metropolitan Vickers, right next to I.C.I. where I worked. So we agreed to take turns driving to work. During this period, I bought an electricity van, an A40. I thought a van would be great for transporting my drum set to various jobs. However, the van turned out to be another problem vehicle. The shock absorbers at the front were no good, and the result was that the passengers would bounce up and down. I didn't mind this too much, but Mr. Starling did. After a couple of trips in the van, he insisted on using his own vehicle from then on.

During my time at I.C.I., one of the directors of our pharmaceutical division visited the University of Wisconsin in the U.S. While he was there, he met Dr. Dale Wurster, who showed him an experiment involving the spraycoating of tablets using a fluid bed drier technique. On his return to I.C.I., he came into our lab, drew a sketch of what he had seen on the back of a table napkin, and said, "See what you can do with that." The conventional way of covering tablets with a sugar coating was long and tedious, taking several days to complete. If tablets could be film coated using a fluid bed dryer, the whole process would be much faster, and the tablets very much lighter.

Taking up the challenge, we conducted experiments using a spray and a six-inch diameter vertical glass tube. Then we went with a 12-inch tube with some success. However, when we tried an 18-inch tube to increase capacity, we encountered many attendant problems. Among other things, we had to move to Macclesfield works, where we could occupy a much larger area. In 1960, there were no electronic controls; so the process was mostly manual.

Wurster tablet coating machine.

The increase in size required special design for several reasons, including the use of flammable solvents; and later, of antistatic bands. To control the rate of spraying on the solvent mix, we had to obtain a large forge blower from Buffalo, New York to lift the 50 kilograms of tablets, along with the stainless steel and Teflon pumping system. The advantage of this system was that there was no increase in the size of the tablets and the coating time was only 20 minutes for 50 kilograms of tablets. Afterwards, printing could be done on the surface of the cellulose, using a machine to do the printing. This project—from the six-inch glass tube to the production-size model—took three years of my time and full attention.

Somewhere along the way, I got fed up with working at I.C.I. My dad had a friend named Walter Bennett, who had started a business selling motor spares at a shop in the Manchester area. Dad told him that I had thought of doing something like that and took me to see him. I was quite impressed with his operation. He had a large stock of parts and a proper business. When English cars first came out after the War, they were sold to the Middle East and the Mediterranean area with no spare parts, and the major automobile companies never followed up with spare parts. Walter's business was to acquire spare parts or substitute spare parts and sell them wherever they were needed. He promised my father that if I ever needed anything, just to ring him up and he would get it for me.

Meanwhile, I began to look around at car dealerships. One day, a dealer asked me if I would like to buy his business. When I asked him what type of business it was and where it was located, he replied, "It's an auto spares business in Samuel Street, Macclesfield." It turned out that he sold spares just like Walter Bennett, only on a smaller scale—sort of like Halfords or Canadian Tire. When I expressed interest, he insisted on introducing me to his partner. The business consisted of a little shop where he worked, and a scrap yard, operated by his employees. His partner's name was Gazillian, and when I saw him I thought he looked familiar. Then I remembered where I had met him before—in a car dealership in Manchester. I decided that I had better make sure the deal was on the up and up and that everything was done properly. I asked Mr. Ashworth, a solicitor, to draw up the deal to make sure there was no funny business. Gazillian agreed, but said we'd have to go down to Albert Square in Manchester to sign the papers. When we arrived, there were several lawyers on hand. While I waited, they chatted freely, not knowing who I was. I decided that they were bigger rogues than the poor devils they were trying to defend. At any rate, we got the whole thing drawn up properly with a guarantee that they wouldn't start a similar business within five miles for five years.

Thus I became the owner my own business, a little shop and a scrap yard. Sheila looked after the shop during the week, selling brake linings and mufflers, some of them stored on the second floor, and calling on Walter Bennett for assistance, as needed. Because we dealt with many types of cars, Sheila became the best parts person in the community. The business did okay, but not well enough for me to leave my job at I.C.I. So I worked in the lab through the week, and on weekends I would work in the scrap yard. Sometimes, Alf White, a band member friend, would come over from Whaley Bridge and help me. We spent quite a bit of time organizing the yard, which was a mess when I purchased the business.

I owned numerous cars during this period, Standards and Daimlers. The best one of all was a 1930 Sunbeam that Roger Starling found in a barn somewhere. It looked like a Rolls Royce, with a grey, aluminum body and a black hard-top vinyl roof. It had 20-inch spoked wheels, a big spare wheel on the running board, and a fog lamp at the front. It had a crash gearbox (non synchromesh). If I missed the gears when I was coming to a stoplight, I would have to stop completely before I could get back into first gear. The original engine was bad, but I managed to replace it with one found in Altringham, a big in-line six overhead valve. The car had an electric starter, but also a hand-crank starter; so if the battery went flat, I could wind it up in front.

1930 Sunbeam.

The inside of the car was also unusual. The front seat was flat right across, with the gear shift change and hand brake positioned next to the door on the driver's side. The back seat, too, was as wide as the car, with plenty of leg room. The carpeted floor was flat, with no prop-shaft tunnel. Moreover, the carpet was removable, as were the floor boards (5/8-inch plywood). So you could walk either side of the prop shaft and perform any maintenance that was necessary. On the steering column was a lever for adjusting the spark and the idle mixture, and you could always set these controls at the optimum position for an easy hand start. You could also set the ignition advanced or back, and the slow running throttle control was also on the lever. I found these features quite useful in bad weather or with poor batteries. The car had a number of other interesting features, including hydraulic brakes, a tinted visor and louvres on the radiator for controlling the flow of air. The hood opened from the side, making it easy to reach the generator and water pump for maintenance. There was even a little compartment under the hood for storing tools.

I drove this car for quite awhile, travelling to Scotland, Wales and the Lake District with Sheila and the children. When we travelled in it, we were literally "riding high;" we could look right over the top of any Morris Minor that happened to be on the road in front of us. The Sunbeam had 12-inch headlights, and had been built by a private company in Wolverhampton in 1930—the same company that built Sir Henry Segrave's Golden Arrow and his Sunbeam. Unfortunately circumstances caused me to sell it in a panic. It was the time of the Suez Crisis, when Nasser was threatening to close up the Suez Canal. I was worried about being able to get enough petrol to get back and forth to work each day; so I sold it.

Barmouth, Wales: Jackie & Rodger in sailboat.

Barmouth Wales: Jackie and Rodger at the beach.

Chapter VIII

It was 1965 when Sheila and I began to consider the possibility of emigrating to Canada. By this time our children, Jacqueline and Rodger, were away from home, Jackie at teacher's college and Rodger at university in Exeter. I had some money saved up from an insurance policy—enough to pay for my return airfare and a trial visit. I said nothing to anyone at work other than my friend Roland Parkinson. However, Sheila and I did discuss it with my brother, David; and Harry Joule, a friend who had lived in Kingston Ontario where he had operated a construction business. After thrashing the project around, we decided to give it a try.

First Sheila and I went to Canadian Immigration to have our health checked and to inquire about jobs. Next I cashed in my insurance policy and purchased a return airline ticket for a one-week visit to Canada. My only flying experience had been in the R.A.F. aboard Lockheed Hudsons, Swordfish, Blackburn Rocks and Walrus Amphibians. So when I boarded a Bocing 707, a four-engine jet plane, at Ringway Airport, it seemed enormous to me.

Once I was aboard, my Canadian adventure got off to a rather bad start. First of all, we took off in a thick fog that continued as we landed at Glasgow. Next, one of the passengers suffered a heart attack, delaying our departure while the baggage handlers fished his luggage off the plane. Eventually, however, we did commence our transatlantic flight. I found the 707 to be a good plane, and we landed safely in Montreal, where we went through Canadian customs.

Our next stop—and my ultimate destination—was Toronto. There I was met by Jim Jarvie, a ham radio operator I had been corresponding with from England. He had sent me information, as well as copies of the *Toronto Star*, which I found very helpful for learning the prices of houses, food and cars. I had even written to him and his partner asking for a job. This turned out to be a bit of a laugh, because their business was just two guys working out of a basement. At any rate, Jim met me at the airport. We had never met, but there was something in his approach that told me he was the person I was looking for. He had booked a hotel room, though a rather expensive one, and I was on a tight budget. Moreover, I noticed during our meal that he ate very little, but drank one beer after another—continuing until almost midnight. By this point I was extremely tired, as I had been awake just about around the clock. However, Jim was still going strong. Pulling a whiskey flask from his hip pocket, he asked if I would like a night cap. I replied, "No, thanks," and stood by the window watching the traffic go up and down Highway 401. I didn't sleep at all that night.

The next morning we went into the city to the area around Yonge and Dundas Streets, looking for a cheaper hotel. We did find a place, and I asked at the desk if I could book a room for the night.

"With a bath?"

"No, I washed before I left."

"It's the only one I have."

"Okay."

"That's five bucks."

"So with no bath, it will be three bucks."

When Jim and I proceeded to the room, we found it dingy and dirty. However, when an old woman with a straw broom entered and began to sweep the carpet, causing dust to fly everywhere, I said, "That's fine; that's fine." At this point Jim left me to go back to work in Sterling, Ontario.

Now it was time for me to start looking for work. Unfortunately it was Friday night on Thanksgiving weekend. (Pity I hadn't known about this when I made my travel arrangements.) I quickly discovered that nothing was open until Tuesday morning. Outside the hotel I could hear a lot of traffic, with cars and taxis pulling up to the traffic lights. I could also hear people going up and down the stairs and a noisy band down in the basement. When I went down to investigate, I found a raucous bar with guys drinking and bouncers doing their job. A guy not far from me said something—I couldn't hear anything offensive in it—and the next thing I knew the bouncers had pitched him into the street. I thought to myself, "This is a really good start."

The next day I located another hotel, the Ford, a bit more expensive, but clean and better looking. As my first interview was scheduled for Tuesday, I decided to rent a car and visit Niagara Falls—just in case I never returned to Canada. However, the holiday weekend made even this nearly impossible, as I wasn't able to rent anything until Sunday, and then only a little Volkswagon. You can just imagine me driving down the Queen Elizabeth Way (Q.E.W.) through Thanksgiving weekend traffic to Niagara Falls. Not only did I have to drive on the "wrong side of the road;" I also had to adjust to the gear shift being on the "wrong side." I did make it to the Falls, however, and it was almost dark when I arrived back in Toronto. Although I more or less knew the way to my hotel, I needed gas, and I wasn't sure where to find the gas tank (it was in the front) or how to release the hood. Somehow I managed.

The following Tuesday, I went for my interview with British Drug Houses (B.D.H.), now Glaxo. I was shown to the president's office where I met a couple of men and a pharmacist. When they asked me where I had stayed and I answered, "The Warwick," they burst out laughing. I guess in Toronto the Warwick was considered to be bottom of the barrel. The interview itself went badly. First I was questioned by the pharmacist, and then they took me around the plant where they were doing development work. It was awful. They were doing things in the old, old, way. Perhaps I shouldn't have said that I had done this, that, or the other. I could see the pharmacist didn't like it and didn't want me around. In short, I didn't get the job.

Later that day I went to my second and third interviews. Once they were over, I thought, "What do I do now? I've still got the rest of the week." So I started going through the Yellow Pages, circling all the chemical companies and phoning them for interviews. I told them where I was staying and that I had come from England looking for a job. I continued this process for four days, during which I managed to get thirteen interviews in four working days. I even delayed my flight for one day to work in a couple of extra interviews.

One of these interviews was with a company in Guelph called Hart Chemicals. At the time, I wasn't familiar with Highway 401, which was not yet finished; so I drove back down the Queen Elizabeth Way (Q.E.W.) to Hwy 6, and then north on Hwy 6 to Guelph. I had to flog my little Volkswagon a bit, but I did manage to get there on time. When I arrived at the Board Room, I was met by a whole flock of people. I felt hot and flustered, but tried to appear calm as they took turns firing questions at me. I must have managed to give some good answers, although they didn't hire me then and there. Instead, a man named Lionel Cooper promised to telephone me in Toronto with their decision. When the call came, he offered me $5,800. I said it wasn't enough and asked for $6,000. He promised to call back. When he did, he told me they had agreed to go for $6,000; so I asked them to send a letter of confirmation to me in England.

Next I caught my Sunday return flight home. At one point, I felt the plane make a sudden dive. As it went down and down, I knew what was happening. It was on auto and had hit an air pocket. "Come on," I thought, "Pull it out, pull it out." When we finally arrived at the airport in Manchester, it was Monday morning. My friend Roland Parkinson, the only one other than Sheila who knew where I had gone, met me at the airport and took me straight to work. When the others asked where I had been for my holiday, I replied, "Not far."

When the letter of confirmation arrived from Hart Chemicals, Sheila and I tossed the situation back and forth within the family for awhile. Eventually, we decided to take the chance; so I telephoned Hart Chemicals and offered to start in December. When they called back, they suggested I wait until the New Year—January 1966. In the meantime Sheila and I had lots to do. Our house was full of furniture. However, we decided not to sell anything for twelve to fourteen months, just in case things didn't work out.

And so I began work with Hart Chemicals in Guelph, Ontario. The plant was big and hot, with steam everywhere, and I was required to wear a hard hat and steel-toed boots. I found that I was able to manipulate the equipment well enough, but the work involved all new stuff—new chemistry. Also I had to hoist 40-gallon drums weighing 400 lbs. onto a dolly, which was difficult for me, not being very tall. All in all I think I did reasonably well. However, Hart Chemicals turned out to be a dangerous place to work. First of all, they made ethylene oxide extractions, which are quite explosive. Secondly, the plant itself was old. It had originally been owned by a private person, and now it was being held together by string and baling wire. I had also heard that the current owner, Manny Bermbaum, was about to sell it to Lever Bros.

In spite of these poor working conditions, I enjoyed the people at the plant. Once a month, they would have a social get-together at the Wellington Hotel in Guelph where we would play darts. However, it was a cold place with a tiled floor—not very joyful. After a couple of evenings there, I suggested we go into Toronto for our next social occasion. They agreed. So we drove into Toronto and down Yonge Street, which in those days was pretty quiet. (During my time at the Ford Hotel, I had had a chance to check out the various places of entertainment in the area.) First I took them to Le Coq D'Or Tavern, where we ordered a drink. At one point, I lit the cigarette for a young woman sitting nearby, and shortly afterwards she got up and entered a brass cage, where she began to dance. A go-go girl, no less!

We went to a couple more places, and then I suggested the Warwick. I thought that place would open their eyes a bit. So there we were—ten or twelve guys from Guelph—running on foot down Dundas St. in Toronto, heading for the Warwick. When we arrived at the entrance, the bouncer asked how many we were. When I answered, "twelve," he motioned us to go up back—into "the gods" as I called them. I slipped him a two-dollar bill and told him I had brought these guys to see the show. So he cleared chairs for us right in front of the stage. Once we were seated and had ordered a round of drinks, the show came on. The girls were only a few feet from us, and my friends' eyes popped out like organ stops. We had a good time at the Warwick, following which we returned to our cars without incident. On the way back to Guelph, one of the guys said, "You've only been here about five months, and yet you know where to go!" Our trip to the big city had been fun and had broken the ice a little.

As I mentioned earlier, I enjoyed the people at Hart Chemicals, but not the plant, which I knew to be unsafe. Once during my time there, we had a minor disaster. It involved a chemical process with hydrochloric acid coming off as fumes. Normally we would feed the fumes into a bucket of ammonia where they would be neutralized and then they would be piped outside through a tube. One day as I approached the big sliding door to the plant, I noticed what at first appeared to be mist or smoke. Then I realized it was hydrochloric acid fumes, which were spreading out over the parking lot—and all over everybody's good paint job. I rushed inside and closed the valves, shut the whole process down. Nobody ever found out about that particular incident. However, people did seem to know the plant wasn't safe. For example, Bell Canada used to store poles in our yard. When they needed some, they would rush in and out as fast as they could. I stayed at Hart Chemicals for only six months. However, they gave me a good send-off. Not long after I left, I heard they had had an explosion that killed one person and injured seventeen.

My next job was in London, Ontario at B.T.I. Canada Duphar, located across from the London Gardens. It was a new plant, and at the time was owned by Labatts. I guess they thought they would go into pharmaceuticals, but they didn't know anything about them. They knew only about brewing beer. The plant had been designed with eight-foot ceilings—totally inadequate to house the large vessels required for the chemicals. You couldn't get a stirrer in a vessel with a clearance of only eight feet. I worked in the development lab, where new products were created. The pharmacist in charge was an Englishman named Tony Beck, and we got along very well. At first I did a bit of work on the bench; next I went to the tablet-making department, where I worked on chloramphenicol, an antibiotic. However, when I developed a rash I learned that I was allergic to chloramphenicol; so I switched to working on other products. Eventually Labatts sold the business to Bristol Myers, who decided to do their future research in Syracuse, New York. We were given one month to find another job. Then Bristol Myers began to cut other staff—using a "hatchet man" to make the company look profitable so they could turn around and sell it.

So at age 46 or 47, I began looking for another job. I found one with W.E. Saunders, an old London pharmaceutical plant with an office on Richmond Street. When I say "old," I mean old. The plant was founded in 1897, and I soon discovered that they hadn't changed much since then. It was an old plant with old people who had old ideas. My job was supposed to be developing new products. Just as I was about to accept this position, Bristol Meyers asked me to stay on with them. In retrospect, I should have accepted their offer because I would have done very well. However, I was uncertain about my future with them; and so I decided to go with Saunders.

It turned out that the Food and Drug people had inspected the plant and had threatened to close it. When they spoke to me, I said, "Look, just give me a year to try and straighten things out. I'll do what I can, and in the meantime, I'll tell you exactly what is happening." Prior to this the company had been bamboozling— covering up just to keep the plant going. The Food and Drug people agreed to let me try. So I had to start changing everything in the plant: the production line, the way they were making things, quality control—the whole works. So instead of becoming Development Manager, I became Plant Manager. From time to time I went to Ottawa, and I became quite friendly with the people there. They trusted me because I always told them the way it really was, whereas they had been led up the garden path before.

Saunders had a lot of old, old products, some of them with formulas that "came out of the Ark." I think I cleared about 200 products out of the line in the first few months. They weren't worth making. Eventually we had a reasonable line going, a decent catalogue and new labelling on the products. We experienced a bit of a hiatus with the labeling because it now had to be in both French and English; the same with the catalogue. Sorting it out involved a lot of working into the night, as well as during the day, but I did eventually succeed.

Meanwhile our president, who had been in the Armed Forces during the war, had met Garfield Weston, the owner of Weston bakeries. Eventually Weston bought out Saunders. The idea was that Saunders would produce the products and Tamblyn Drugs (which already belonged to Weston) would retail them— something like Boots in England. It seemed to be a good idea. However, the purchasing agent for Tamblyn was the type who had to have everything his own way. He was an obdurate man with a chip on his shoulder; so what could have been a good arrangement wasn't working. So the next time Ted Craven, the president of Saunders, called on Garfield Weston in England, Weston told him to sell the company.

Eventually it was sold to an American Company. However, they were not in pharmaceuticals either; they made turbine blades for aircraft engines. What they were doing was buying up small pharmaceutical companies in the U.S. and Canada, putting them all together, and selling them as a "job lot" for a substantial profit. I suggested they get out of their old building, move into a smaller space, and get new products going. When I told them about my experiences at I.C.I., they weren't interested. They just wanted to sell the company for profit.

Finally they did sell to someone in Detroit. Sandy, our Accountant; Ted Craven, our President; and I had to travel to Detroit and sit in front of this objectionable man—like little school boys in a row—while he gave us hell. When I couldn't stand it any longer, I stood up and walked around to HIS side of the desk and told him what was going on, while the other two just sat there—scared stiff.

Just as I started to get on reasonably well with the people in St. Louis, who also worked in small pharmaceutical companies, our company was sold, and the nephew of the Detroit man decided to move the business to Toronto. They were going to close the plant and lay off all the staff. One man had been there nearly 30 years, and his wife, 25 years. They were going to be laid off with only two weeks' pay. I told them they couldn't do that. I demanded they give them money for each year of service with the plant. We had a big meeting in a penthouse near Toronto Airport with men from St. Louis and other places. It was 1973, in the Trudeau era, and there was an election pending. I told them that foreign ownership was a "hot potato;" that I knew people in high places; and that YOU KNOW WHAT would come down heavily on them, if they didn't provide adequate compensation for the staff. In the end, I didn't get as much as I wanted, but I did get compensation for each year of service for all the people at the plant. This, of course, left me at loose ends as well.

Our production manager, Tony Dunbar, had recently been married to a girl from Ireland. I advised him to take a week off and to go up one side of the 401 and down the other until he had found a job. He did find one with Park Davis in Brockville. Meanwhile, one of our salesmen, whom we called "Boom Boom" because he had such a loud voice, had moved to a London Ontario Real Estate company and asked me to come and join them. I decided to give it a try.

So I took the Real Estate course in Stratford, travelling each day through the winter months until I had earned my certificate. I enjoyed the course and soon discovered that I liked the business as well. Unfortunately the money just wasn't there. If I listed a house, somebody else would sell; after which a quarter would go to my broker; a quarter to myself and the rest to the other salesman and his broker. I would end up with only 25 per cent; yet I had done all the running around and burning of gas. So I decided to look elsewhere.

I was a member of the Chemical Institute of Canada (C.I.C.) and treasurer of the local branch. I had also served as chairman while I was working for Saunders. As a result, I knew quite a few people from the University of Western Ontario (U.W.O.). One day, one of them asked if I would like to work at the university, and I said, "Yes." So I went to work there and stayed for about three years. It was a secure job—absolutely secure—but also miserable. Having been chairman of the Chemical Society and Plant Manager for Saunders, I found it was quite a comedown to attend the labs for first-year chemistry students. However, my own pride made me do a good job. Of course, there was another reason: my son Rodger was at the University at the time, completing his Ph.D.; and I didn't want to cause any fuss. Nevertheless I hated the job. I would sit at lunch with all the professors, some of whom I had known before, and would see that they knew nothing of the outside world, nothing at all. They would bicker and quarrel and tittle-tattle. It was quite pathetic.

In the meantime, I knew a radio ham who worked in the photochemical department, just down the corridor. I asked him if there were any openings at his end. He promised to check, but never did. However, I did eventually have an interview with the photochemical people. Because I had a lot of radio and electronic knowledge, they put me in charge of ordering all the components for these intense arc lamp systems that were being developed at the University. They were good guys, but eventually they had to leave the campus, as they were selling things commercially to outside companies, and were not allowed to do that from the campus.

They called their business Photochemical Research Associates (P.R.A.), and I went with them. At first they put me in charge of production. Next I went on to do budgeting and costing: I did time studies on the hours of assembling certain equipment and the cost of the component parts. I also ordered parts from outside the plant. The president was a Hungarian, who spent a lot of time travelling in Europe. I used to see his American Express bills, and I knew that the things he was ordering were not for his stereo equipment—as he was claiming. After some investigation, I realized that the equipment was being shipped to Russia via Vienna, and at the time Russia was not Canada's friend.

I found myself in a quandary. Should I call the R.C.M.P. or what should I do? Rodger was still in university, and I didn't want the whole hill of beans coming down on both our heads. At about the same time, we had a break-in at the premises, and our president, the Hungarian, was in quite a tizzy. Of course, I knew why. I decided I had better get out; so I called Surinda, an acquaintance who was just starting with a company, and he hired me to help start a new plant.

The plant was to make electronic gadgets that took the load off an electric motor when it was starting up. It was an energy-saving device. I began to order some of the equipment for the plant and insertion equipment for the components to go in. I also interviewed about 40 women as potential employees, and we had some very expensive equipment delivered. At one point, a man from Phillips Electronics asked me if I was sure this operation was all right. I answered, "Yes, as far as I know." However, one day when I reported for work, I was handed a pay cheque and told that it would be my last. The whole thing had been a scam.

Apparently a London insurance agent had some local medical doctors as clients and had told them he knew a way they could make a lot more money than they could with their current investments. The scam involved a hotel in Goderich, a holiday camp in Haliburton, an iron works in East London, and also our plant in London, Ontario. He had been putting the money in and moving it around so that all these enterprises appeared to be doing well, when in fact they were not. Eventually the bubble burst and the whole thing collapsed. District Trust, then of London, had put $11 million into it. As a result they went "belly up" and their accountant was put on the hot seat for involving them in this. Meanwhile, the insurance agent who had started the whole thing got off and kept his nice big house in Orangeville, whereas some of our employees had mortgaged their houses to put money into the scam.

So here I was again, 50 odd years of age, with no job and a house to pay for—after a very checkered career! One day I happened to run into Russ Robinson, a member of the C.I.C. and he asked me what I was currently doing. When I replied, "Nothing," he asked what had happened and I gave him an outline of the story. Then he told me the Department of Agriculture was looking for someone and asked if I'd like to apply. He said he would get the forms and tell me what to say and what not to say. For example, I wasn't to mention my various positions of responsibility, because this was just a laboratory job.

So I filled in all the forms and entered the competition. There were three or four of us—two being recent graduates. However, I got the job, as I think they were looking for someone more mature who could handle the electronic equipment for gas analysis. Also, Russ Robinson wanted to unload the radioactive responsibility to someone. They were using radioactive isotopes in the labs, and so keeping them in order and under control was important. Russ and I got along fine. We had both been in the Air Force, and we would talk about it as we did our experiments. Our experimental work was with flies. As I had been in West Africa and dealt with mosquitoes, I had some knowledge of entomology. That stood me in good stead as well. In fact, we published a paper in the *American Journal of Biochemistry*. (My name had been in print before when I worked at I.C.I. in England.)

I remained with the Department of Agriculture for about two and one-half years before retiring in 1984. It was a happy time because I got along fine with everybody. Of course it took a while for me to get to know the others and for them to get to know me. Many of them were academics, and I was not. It was a pretty straightforward job, not a great hassle, but I had to pay attention to what I was doing, especially with the radioactive isotopes. Once I even had to tell one of the chemists what not to do, "Don't splash it about, Mister." Nevertheless I learned a lot there—occupational therapy, I might say.

Chapter IX

My story would be incomplete without an account of my various automobiles and recreational pursuits following our move to Canada in 1966. As my first Canadian job was in Guelph, Ontario, I needed a car to get to work. Although there were city buses, the service wasn't very good; and if I travelled by bus out of the city, I had trouble making connections. At the time, it was also important for me to have a good look around Ontario before deciding whether to stay in Canada and sell our house in England.

I needed wheels, but I didn't have much money. When I made the rounds of the various car dealerships, I found the prices out of my reach. Then one dealer asked what I was looking for and said, "I know where there is a car for sale on a back street in Toronto." The car turned out to be a 1958 Chevrolet, all painted yellow. It was January, and I didn't have a chance to look underneath the vehicle. Nonetheless, I bought it for $300 and named it the "Yellow Peril." It was long and straight, with a six cylinder engine, and I soon discovered that it was worthy of the name I had given it. Underneath, it was terribly rusty, and although the engine ran, it did not run very well. At the time, I was billeted with a couple named Con and Irene Steele, both of them six feet tall. When they got into the back seat of my car, they had to be extremely careful to avoid going right through the floor. Moreover, the first time I reached for the emergency brake, it came off into my hand. I had discovered that Con was a fairly good mechanic; so the two of us took the cylinder head off and got the engine running reasonably well. I recall travelling with Con to nearby Fergus and returning to Guelph with great trepidation during a snowstorm. We barely made it back.

In spite of all this, I kept the Chevrolet for awhile. Easter was coming up when I would have a chance to see some more of Ontario. Of course, I had no idea of distances in Canada. I planned to drive from Guelph to Sarnia, cross into the U.S., motor to Detroit and re-enter Ontario at Windsor. As I drove along Hwy 22, I thought I must be travelling all the way to Canada's West Coast, the highway seemed so long. I was beginning to realize how big Ontario is—never mind Canada.

When I finally reached Detroit, I couldn't believe the number of cars in the city. There were lines and lines of them, street after street. I thought, "This must be why they call it the Motor City." When I reached the city centre, I booked a hotel, and went into a bar to order a drink and watch the show. When I left, the streets looked deserted and I noticed that the police were walking in pairs. The next morning I headed for Windsor. When I stopped for gas, I discovered a pool of oil under the car. I knew that either the main bearings of the engine—or the seals on the main bearing at the back of the engine—were gone. In January when I had purchased the car, the oil would have been reasonably thick; now with the warmer weather, I could clearly see that the main bearings were in deep trouble.

Shortly after I returned to Guelph, I traded the Chevy in for a 1958 Rambler, a medium-sized car, and very comfortable to ride in. It had an automatic gear shift, with a push button on the left side of the dash which you used to change from first, to second and third gear—very convenient. However, as soon as I left the dealer's lot, the engine started to make a terrible noise; so I turned around and drove back. The dealer listened to the engine, removed the sump, and redid the big end bearings—all at no charge.

This Rambler's engine proved to be gutless. Although it was a straight six, I think it must have been a G.M. throw out. Nevertheless, I continued to drive it. For one thing, I could sleep in this car as the passenger seat in the front folded down flat. This enabled me to continue my rambles around Ontario. On one trip, I went to Owen Sound. When I arrived there, I learned that I couldn't get a drink, as it was a "dry" town. On Sunday morning radio, all I could find was church music, and I personally counted thirteen churches in the city. Another time, I travelled to Collingwood. I also drove to Niagara Falls, which I had visited on my first trip to Canada. This time the temperature was 104 degrees Fahrenheit, and my engine boiled over. I managed to get home by stopping frequently and filling the radiator with cool water. At the time I didn't know about using anti-freeze to raise the boiling point of the radiator fluid.

When I noticed the Rambler was beginning to rust, I traded it for a G.M. Strato Chief, a fairly large car with a long six engine. I had seen these engines before and remember thinking, "You can never wear those engines out with normal driving." As a matter of fact, I don't remember any serious mechanical problems with this engine. When Jackie came from England for Christmas in 1966, we were still driving the Strato Chief. The following year, when our son Rodger came for a visit, we decided to find out what it was like pulling a trailer on Canadian roads. (In England we had done some trailering with a heavily built caravan.) So we put a tow bar on the Strato Chief, rented a small trailer named Rocket, and headed for Expo 67 in Montreal. At the time, I was working for a company owned by Labatt's, and had been told that we could park on the Labatt grounds in Montreal. I expected the grounds to be nice, with flower beds and green grass. Instead we found ourselves in a paved yard behind a brewery, with constant steam and noise. We did get to Expo, however, and enjoyed it very much. Then we headed south into Vermont, where unfortunately, the trailer hitch got stuck on the hump of a railway crossing. With no extra springing in the Strato Chief, the hitch was pretty low. Eventually, following a struggle, we managed to get off the crossing. It was difficult as the Strato Chief had a stick shift, not an automatic. At our next stop, Lake Bomoseen, I had trouble manoeuvring into a small space. In fact, as I backed up slowly, I saw smoke rising through the floor boards. The clutch was slipping and burning.

We left the trailer at Bomoseen and went to visit a friend, Mike Fisher, who had worked with me in the I.C.I. at Blakely, England. He had left England before I did and had landed a very good job at Merck in Rahway, just outside of New York City. While we were there, we decided to visit the Big Apple. We drove into the city and found the streets full of potholes. Our poor old car was shaken to pieces. After going to the top of the Empire State Building and enjoying a meal, we headed back to Mike's for one more night before returning to Bomoseen to pick up our trailer. The Strato Chief pulled it with no problem, and we found towing in Canada and the U.S. to be a breeze compared to towing in the U.K. Most of the roads in North America are wide and straight, whereas in the U.K., many are twisty, narrow and steep.

Following this adventure, we decided to buy our own trailer, and began to look around. We soon found one in a nice handy size, a Corsair, which for some reason had not quite been completed. Either something had happened at the factory where it was being built, or the manufacturer had gone bankrupt. So we bought it for a good price. By this time we had purchased a Pontiac with automatic transmission; so we had no trouble manoeuvring it. When Jackie and Maurice came for a visit, we took them to Vermont, and had no problems. We had this trailer for eleven years and towed it with a number of different cars.

Finger Lakes 1979: Catalina with the *Caroline* on top and pulling the Corsair.

In 1968 or 1969, Rodger came over from England to study for his Ph.D. in chemistry at the University of Western Ontario. By then, Sheila and I were living in Lambeth where there was no convenient bus route to the University. So Rodger needed a car. We went to a dealership where we saw a 1961 Ford Fairlane. It was a six cylinder, but it had no guts at all. When we test drove it, it sounded terrible. Rodger and I opened the hood and discovered that somebody had put the plug leads on in the wrong place. We went back to the dealer and said, "Look, this sounds terrible. We can't give you much money for this." He sold it to us for $275.00. It was an old car with a cracked windshield, but a friend who worked at Speedy Autoglass came over one afternoon with a spare windshield and installed it in 20 minutes while he enjoyed a cup of tea. So Rodger now had a car.

The next thing was to teach him to drive, as he had never learned. We found a suitable school yard for practice and got started. I gave him a crash course—without crashing the car. He passed his test; and so was able to drive back and forth to the University.

Not long afterwards, we moved to Komoka and Sheila got a job at the London, Ontario Metropolitan Store in the shoe department. At first she rode to work with a co-worker; but this lady was a terrible driver and Sheila would be a nervous wreck by the time she got to work. She had seen me teach Rodger to drive, and she decided that she would like lessons too. We decided that she should drive the Fairlane and Rodger could drive my car to work. We found another school yard and repeated the crash course. When the time came, Sheila passed her test, and the Fairlane served her very well until one day, on her way home from work, a woman ran into the back of her car while she was stopped for a school bus. As a result, her car was no longer driveable.

Fortunately, a policeman on a motor bike had seen the accident, and no blame was attached to Sheila. So we got the claims forms from All State, the woman's insurance company, and submitted them. All State tried to get away with paying only a pittance for our wrecked car, but we insisted that Sheila have a car of equal value. They gave us a rented car for a month. They also gave us a cash settlement and allowed us to keep the wreck. I knew that the engine was valuable, as we had put it in just a few weeks prior to the accident. We managed to sell the wreck, and we replaced it with an eight-cylinder Chevrolet for about $300.00. Sheila drove this for quite awhile, back and forth to the nursing home where she was working at the time. Eventually it too rusted out.

Sheila's next car was a 1972 Buick Skylark, with a 350 cubic inch V8 engine, in good condition. I wasn't sure about it, as it was a very fast, sporty looking vehicle. We began to call Sheila "Stirling Moss," as she would turn off the main road into Kilworth St., Komoka, and spin gravel—I mean really spin gravel. We drove this car to Florida twice, and it did very well. In fact, on one of these trips, I was sick and Sheila drove most of the way home. However, on the second trip, the car started to get really noisy, so I went to a Florida dealer and exchanged it for a 1980 Buick Century. I knew that in Florida they don't salt the roads and so rust wouldn't be a problem.

While I was working for Saunders, a pharmaceutical company, I had the opportunity to purchase company cars that were coming off a two-year lease. On one occasion, I flew to Montreal to pick up one of these cars. The dealer held me up for so long that I was unable to purchase license plates before the local office closed. As a result, I drove all the way to Kingston and then all the way home after dark without any plates. Our trailer-towing problems were solved when we bought both a GM truck with a camper top and trailer from a man who did a lot of fishing. We subsequently drove many miles with our truck and trailer around the Eastern U.S.A.

At the time of my retirement in 1984, Sheila and I were living in Komoka. Almost immediately afterwards, while visiting friends in Tweed, Ontario, we saw a house that we liked on Stoco Lake; so we decided to sell our house in Komoka and buy it. Sailing had been one of our hobbies in England, and we had also enjoyed sailing in Canada on Lakes Erie and Huron. In fact, I had a custom-made steel keel for our sailboat, which gave it greater stability. So we continued to enjoy sailing in Tweed for many years.

Tweed, Ontario, 1974: Peter and Sheila sailing the
***Caroline* on Lake Stoco.**

We also travelled to Florida, staying there for five months in the winter, where I had the opportunity to pursue another of my favourite pastimes, playing with a band. I also continued my work with amateur radio. Over the years, each of our homes, and even our trailers, had been fitted with antennas and housed my radio equipment.

Lambeth, Ontario 1967: Peter and Sheila's first Canadian rental home.

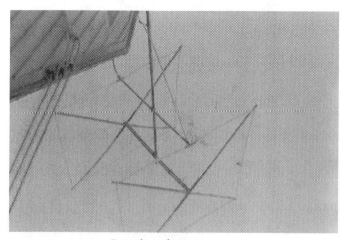

Peter's radio antenna.

Vermont c. 1994: Beatson trailer with radio antenna.

Tweed, Ontario 1985: Raising radio antenna.

In 1992, we bought a trailer in Bradenton, Florida, that was situated on half to three quarters of an acre. On Saturday nights we would go to our park's recreation hall to hear a live band. The band already had a drummer, but when I told the leader I could play the clarinet, he invited me to join them for their Thursday practice. Next I began to play along with them on Saturday nights, making friends with the trombone player, who supported me when I miffed it. I also sat in for the drummer on occasion. Eventually I even had the audacity to play solos in front of the audience. The band would play a tune, and then they'd say, "You take the next chorus." So I would, and strangely enough, I managed—it was a matter of having to manage, as I would be standing in the front line on the stage, with all the people lined up in front of me on the floor. In time, the drummer began to drop out, and I found myself playing the drums more and more. Eventually, I was playing with the band regularly, mostly on drums. Some of the players were from our camp, while others were from outside. Some were very good, while others were terrible. You never knew what you were getting until they showed up. As we were all volunteers, it was difficult to demand that everyone come to practices. Meanwhile, the pianist, who had been playing with the band at the camp for a number of years, decided that he wanted out as band leader. So he asked me to take over. The first year I refused, but when he asked me the next year and really twisted my arm, I agreed to take it on.

Well it was fun, but lots of work. I bought my own set of drums from guy who was quitting to move back up north. He sold me his drums for $300.00. It was a good set, old, but well made by Slingerland. The metal work, stands, and everything else were very substantial. On Saturday nights after we had finished playing, I would stay behind to pack up my drums; and to take down the music stands and lights. The following Monday, I would start on the next week's programme. We didn't want the same tunes every week, so I would vary the programme, depending on what music was available, and we had a fair amount to choose from. By Wednesday, I would have it all drawn out and would make photocopies for each member of the band. At our practice on Thursday morning, we would hash it all out, and then I would have to revise it and make new copies for our performance on Saturday night.

Another task that fell to me was getting players. There weren't enough within the camp to make a band. I'm not talking about a big band—just four or five players. I used to go to the American Legion, where on Sunday afternoons there would be a jam session. Some of the players were very good; so I would go up to them and ask if they would play for us on Saturday night. Their first question would be, "How much?" Then I would have to explain that while we could pay their legitimate expense, we couldn't do much more, as it was a seniors' park. I did manage to co-opt quite a few players this way. If they came on Saturday and enjoyed themselves, they might come again the next Saturday. We developed a nucleus of fairly good players. However, I had trouble finding pianists. Surprisingly, I did find one who lived near the camp. He hailed from Exeter, Ontario, and played with us quite a bit. For awhile, the two of us also played at an adjacent park on Wednesdays, and at another park on Fridays.

Our camp had a nice hall, a good stage, and all the necessary lights and microphones. At first the band didn't charge any admission. People would come in off the street and enjoy two hours of entertainment for nothing. We provided cookies, coffee and soft drinks. We would put out a basket to help defray expenses, but we started losing money as often 90 or 100 people would show up, and many of them did not pay. So we started charging $1.00 at the door. I used some of that money to pay the musicians who had come from outside. At first the Committee objected, but I said that we couldn't expect these musicians to come and play for nothing. So eventually things settled down. By this time I knew that this would be my last season of coming to Florida. Rising medical insurance premiums, plus the cost of our rental were making it impractical. However, I played right up to the end.

Our camp also had a choir, and sometimes I would play the drums for them. They had a piano and about 25 or 30 good singers. However, they sometimes had problems keeping the time and knitting their program together; so I'd play the drums to help them keep the time; I also helped them with their program. At the end of the year they always gave a concert. Once I knew that Sheila and I were enjoying one of our last winters in Florida, I decided to arrange something special. So I put together a program of Broadway tunes over the years. There was a lot to choose from; and I needed information on the various composers to provide some dialogue in between numbers. I obtained information from the Internet on composers like Irving Berlin, Harry Warren, Rogers & Hammerstein, etc. Our pianist's wife had a good speaking voice, and she offered to read the dialogue. A week before the concert, I handed her all my hand-written material, only to discover, on the day before the concert, that her typewriter had broken down. So I went to the Goodwill or Salvation Army, purchased a typewriter for $10.00 and put it on her doorstep at 9:00 a.m. on the day of the concert—just in time for her to type up the dialogue.

I actually spent two years preparing this program: sorting the tunes out, researching, and writing out the appropriate dialogue. Some of the tunes were from Broadway shows, both before World War II and between the Wars. I also included tunes from the present day by composers such as Andrew Lloyd Webber. The show went very well, and someone captured it on video. I still have that video.

The week before we left Florida, I advertised my drums. They were sold by 10:00 o'clock the next morning for $350.00. I'd paid only $300.00 for them and had given them plenty of use. I had also bought a clarinet for $75.00 at a Florida flea market, but I kept the clarinet. I wondered if I'd ever have a chance again to play with a group. I had played in England from 1946 to 1965. Then I hadn't played at all for the next 25 years. I had enjoyed my years of playing in Florida. Only time would tell whether I might play again.

After 18 years living in Tweed, Ontario, Sheila and I decided to relocate. We could no longer spend our winters in Florida, and we were finding it too much to get our sailboat in and out of the water. So we sold the sailboat to a woman from Belleville; next we sold our house and trailer. Finally, we purchased a house in Tillsonburg. We had visited the town before, as our daughter, Jackie, had been living in nearby Brownsville. We liked the shopping and the fact that the town had its own hospital. We made our move to Tillsonburg in the fall of 2003.

Shortly afterwards, I noticed an ad for musicians by a Tillsonburg group called the *Melody Makers*. I joined this group and have been playing with them ever since. Our audiences are the residents of nursing homes and retirement homes in Tillsonburg and the surrounding area. We practise on Mondays and perform several times a month. I play both the drums and the clarinet, but mostly the drums. At the time of writing in 2009, I have been playing with the *Melody Makers* for five years.

Post Script

When Sheila and I made the decision to emigrate to Canada in 1966, our daughter, Jacqueline, was attending teacher's college in Crewe; and our son, Rodger, was attending university in Exeter. So both our children stayed in England to complete their studies.

Before the War, Sheila, had been employed at Lever Bros. in England, where she worked on Hollerith tabulating machines. These machines were the forerunners of present day computers and used a punch-card system. In 1942, Sheila joined the R.A.F. and was subsequently posted to the Air Ministry in London. At this time, London was subject to nightly bombing raids and attacks by V1 and V2 rockets. Sheila was stationed in London until 1945 because of her experience with Hollerith machines, as the R.A.F. was using Power Samis, a similar system, for their records.

After moving to Canada, Sheila, with great tolerance, went along with my various hair-brained schemes and job changes. She learned to drive a car at 47 years of age, took trailer trips with me and the children throughout the U.S, and Canada, and even learned to sail a yacht, where she was a good, competent crew, and unafraid. Sheila and I were married for 64 years. She took great pride in our home, wherever we were, and was a great wife and courageous companion. Sheila passed away in 2007.

Our daughter, Jackie, came to Canada in 1974 with her husband, Maurice, and their two children, Caroline and John. At this time, the rules of admission for teachers had recently changed, and the Ontario educational authorities would no longer accept her qualifications or experience, whereas during the teacher shortage a few years earlier, they would have. As Jackie did not wish to begin her studies all over again, she looked elsewhere for employment, even though she had successfully taught school for four years in the U.K. First she took an assistant's job in a London Ontario pharmacy, a position she enjoyed very much. Subsequently she divided her time, in the same capacity, between two separate hospital pharmacies. Next she served as administrator for a girls' home. Finally, she worked in social services for Elgin County until her retirement in 2002. Jackie and Maurice continue to live in Tillsonburg, Ontario.

Our son, Rodger, came to Canada after obtaining his B.Sc. in chemistry and began post-graduate studies in London, Canada at the University of Western Ontario. Before completing his doctoral program, he took a year off to study in Hong Kong, where he lived with a Chinese family, an experience he found both rewarding and interesting. Returning to Canada, he resubmitted his research proposal and received his Ph.D. Following this he was married to Carolyn and became a father to Ian. In 1990, tempted by a job offer in Vancouver, he purchased a house and moved west. Subsequently, due to some internal political wrangling, Rodger's job was terminated. Today he works as an Instructor for the British Columbia Institute of Technology (B.C.I.T.) and as an Adjunct Professor in the Department of Wood Science at the University of British Columbia (U.B.C.). Rodger occasionally comes to Ontario on business.

Conclusion

Upon my retirement from the Department of Agricultural Research in London, Ontario, in 1984—the formal end of my working life—I had occasion to look back and ask, "What was it all about?" I had met many people in my travels, some famous, some not. However, I had always valued their friendship, no matter what the situation or circumstances.

My hope today is that I have been able to pass on to them—and to you, the reader—some of the lessons that I have learned over time. I also hope I have helped some friends over the humps in life that all of us encounter on our individual journeys.

Peter Beatson, Tillsonburg, Ontario, January 2010